A Baby Blues® Treasury

Baby Blues®

Ten Years and Still in Diapers

Other Baby Blues® books from Andrews McMeel Publishing

Guess Who Didn't Take a Nap?
I Thought Labor Ended When the Baby Was Born
We Are Experiencing Parental Difficulties. . . Please Stand By
Night of the Living Dad
I Saw Elvis in My Ultrasound
One More and We're Outnumbered!
Check, Please. . .
threats, bribes & videotape
If I'm a Stay-At-Home Mom, Why Am I Always in the Car?

Treasury

The Super-Absorbent Biodegradable Family-Size Baby Blues®

A Baby Blues® Treasury

Baby Blues®
Ten Years and Still in Diapers

by Rick Kirkman & Jerry Scott

**Andrews McMeel
Publishing**

Kansas City

www.andrewsmcmeel.com

99 00 01 02 03 BAM 10 9 8 7 6 5 4 3 2 1

ISBN: 0-7407-0008-1

Library of Congress Catalog Card Number: 99-61208

For Kim and Abbey.

—J.S.

To Sukey, my partner in sleep deprivation for a decade and a half—with much love and many thanks.

And to my two (not-so-little-anymore) bundles of joy—Taylor and Maddie,
who have made being their dad the most rewarding experience of my life.

—R.K.

"SQUEAK"

AHA!

GROWN-UP TALK! SYLLABLES! I WANT TO HEAR SYLLABLES! NOW!

KIRKMAN & SCOTT

WHEN MOMS GO BAD.

The thing that strikes us when we look at these early strips is how *Baby Blues* has changed over the past ten years . . . and how much it has remained the same. We were both just learning how to produce a daily comic strip, so the writing and the artwork were a little crude, but the theme of the strip has been simple and strong from the beginning. *Baby Blues* is all about parenting.

SO ANYWAY— THAT'S WHAT WE WANT. WHAT DO YOU THINK? CAN WE? HUH? PULEEEZ?

PHONE

WE CAN? REALLY? WELL, GREAT!! THANKS! YOU WON'T REGRET THIS—I PROMISE!

PHONE

GOOD NEWS! THE BABYSITTER SAID WE CAN STAY OUT ANOTHER HOUR!

PHONE

KIRKMAN & SCOTT

HMMM... ACCORDING TO THIS CHAPTER, WE'RE SUPPOSED TO BE FEELING A REAL SENSE OF CONNECTION WITH OUR BABY BY NOW.

I THINK THEY'RE TALKING **EMOTIONAL** CONNECTION HERE, WANDA.

WHATEVER.

KIRKMAN & SCOTT

Back in 1990, the debate over cotton diapers versus disposable diapers was raging. The environmentalists were telling us that disposables were bad for the environment and babies, while the disposable diaper manufacturers were claiming the opposite. Darryl and Wanda wrestled with the issue and came down on the side of disposables. No political statement was intended . . . it just seemed like a Darryl and Wanda decision. This probably generated as much mail as any issue we've covered in the strip, except breast-feeding.

WE ARE SOCIALLY RESPONSIBLE PEOPLE...

WE DON'T SMOKE, WE RECYCLE ALUMINUM AND NEWSPAPER, WE USE ROLL-ON DEODORANT, AND WE GIVE MONEY TO GREENPEACE.

WE REFUSE TO FEEL GUILTY FOR USING DISPOSABLE DIAPERS, SO JUST CUT US SOME SLACK!!

KIRKMAN & SCOTT

DARRYL, PLEASE...

PAPER OR PLASTIC?

WHAT ARE YOU, SOME KIND OF A WISE GUY!?

IS THAT DADDY'S GIRL? YES, IT IS.

WHAT'S THAT? HUH? IS THAT ZOE? YES, IT IS!

WHATCHA DOING?

OH... I WAS JUST NOTICING HER SOFT SPOT.

THAT'S FUNNY. I WAS JUST ADMIRING YOURS.

ACCORDING TO THIS STUDY, IT NOW COSTS $150,000 TO RAISE A CHILD TO AGE 18.

WOW!

AND THAT DOESN'T INCLUDE COLLEGE! ADD $77,000 FOR FOUR YEARS AT AN IN-STATE PUBLIC UNIVERSITY!

THAT'S SCARY.

THAT'S OUTRAGEOUS!

THAT'S $27,750 A POUND!

KIRKMAN & SCOTT

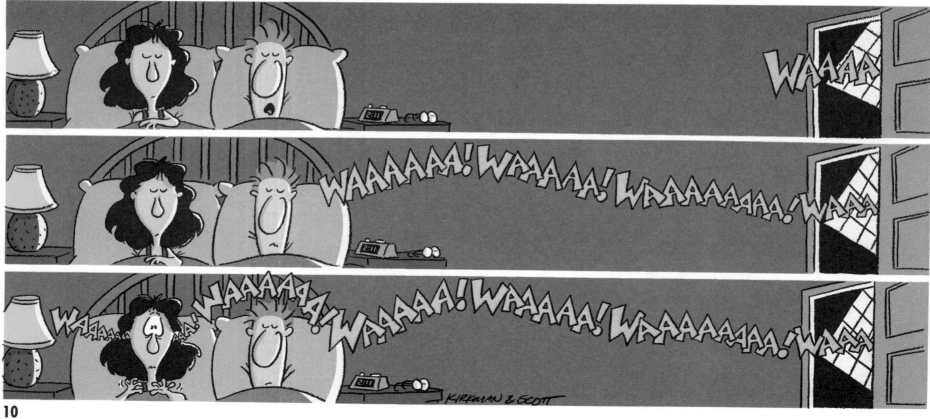

When you're on a first-name basis and have a regular standing appointment with your pediatrician, you know you're in trouble. We did, and we were. —R.K.

Volkswagen was running an extensive advertising campaign in early 1990 using the word "fahrvergnügen" (nobody knows what it even really meant, but somehow it made you want to buy a Volkswagen). We used the word in a strip not remembering that dumb advertising campaigns disappear, but dumb comic strip gags can follow you around in collection books like this one for years. Note to aspiring comic strip artists: Don't do this.

11

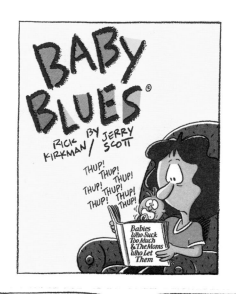

BABY BLUES®

by RICK KIRKMAN / JERRY SCOTT

YOU KNOW, THIS SAYS THAT PACIFIERS AREN'T A VERY GOOD IDEA.

IT SAYS THAT IF A BABY ALWAYS HAS A PACIFIER, IT WILL KEEP HER FROM EXPLORING TOYS AND OTHER OBJECTS WITH HER MOUTH, WHICH IS AN IMPORTANT PART OF HER DEVELOPMENT.

ACCORDING TO THIS, YOU SHOULD TAKE IT AWAY BEFORE THE BABY BECOMES TOO ATTACHED TO IT.

TOO LATE.

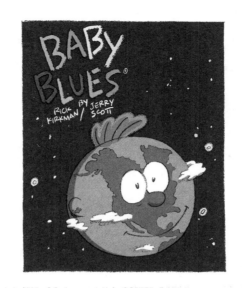

BABY BLUES
by RICK KIRKMAN / JERRY SCOTT

WE NEED TO GET OUT.

EEEEEE

WE'RE SO CAUGHT UP IN OUR OWN LITTLE WORLD THAT WE'RE LOSING TOUCH WITH THE OUTSIDE,

WE NEED TO GO OUT FOR AN EVENING... JUST THE TWO OF US.

THAT SOUNDS GREAT.

WE CAN GET TO KNOW EACH OTHER AGAIN! TALK ABOUT THE NEWS! DISCUSS MOVIES! WE CAN REDISCOVER LIFE OUTSIDE PARENTHOOD!

LET'S DO IT!

KIRKMAN & SCOTT

SO, WHAT DO YOU THINK ZOE IS DOING NOW?

This strip was inspired by a particularly uncooperative kid I saw in the grocery store. —J.S.

We constantly steal ideas from friends and relatives. This one was almost verbatim from a friend in California who was describing her response to her daughter's learning to crawl.

16

POIT!

HERE... LET MOMMY WASH THAT OFF FOR YOU, ZOE.

ZIP!

THERE! ALL BETTER!

RUB RUB RUB

THUP! THUP! THUP! THUP! THUP! THUP!

KIRKMAN & SCOTT

In the early days I had to look no further than our own living room for reference. —R.K.

MacPHERSON PLAYGROUND... MONKEY BARS SPEAKING...

RING!
RING!

KIRKMAN & SCOTT

WANDA, WHERE'S THAT PIZZA COUPON THAT I CUT OUT OF THE PAPER LAST WEEK?

ON THE REFRIGERATOR.

COULD YOU BE MORE SPECIFIC?

KIRKMAN & SCOTT

A portrait of our fridge. Where did they put pictures, comic strips, and coupons before they invented the refrigerator door? —J.S.

OW!

WHAT'S THE MATTER?

I WAS JUST TRYING TO REMEMBER WHAT IT WAS LIKE TO GO FROM THE KITCHEN TO THE LIVING ROOM WITHOUT PULLING A HAMSTRING.

KIRKMAN & SCOTT

It was years before we could go to a movie without calling home from the theater. —R.K.

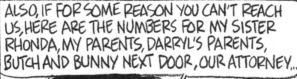

You're never so aware of the evils of the world until you're a parent.

Zoe turned one year old after two years on the comics page. Obviously, syndication is the fountain of youth . . . for the characters, that is.

ZOE, COME HERE AND LET MOMMY CHANGE YOUR DIAPER.

ZOE! WAIT! PLEASE LET MOMMY CHANGE YOUR DIAPER!

PLEASE? PLEASE? PLEASE? PL—

MOTHERHOOD IS THE ONLY OCCUPATION WHERE YOU HAVE TO BEG TO DO SOMETHING THAT YOU DON'T WANT TO DO IN THE FIRST PLACE!

KIRKMAN & SCOTT

ZOE LEARNED A NEW WORD TODAY.

SMOOCH!

REALLY? WHAT WORD? CAN YOU SAY IT FOR DADDY? HUH? CAN YOU? COME ON, SWEETIE, SAY THE WORD! SAY THE WORD! SAY THE WORD!

NO!

MY! SHE SAYS IT WELL!

AND OFTEN.

NO-NO-NO-NO-NO-NO-NO-NO-NO-NO-

KIRKMAN & SCOTT

...HE STUCK IN HIS THUMB AND PULLED OUT A PLUM...

...BAKE ME A CAKE AS FAST AS YOU CAN...

...TOGETHER THEY LICKED THE PLATTER CLEAN!

YOU KNOW WHAT WE NEED? WE NEED SOME NURSERY RHYMES ABOUT AEROBICS.

KIRKMAN & SCOTT

BABY BLUES
BY RICK KIRKMAN / JERRY SCOTT

THAT'S THE FOURTH TIME YOU'VE SEEN THIS VIDEO TODAY...

...CAN DADDY SEE WHAT HAPPENED IN THE **REAL** WORLD TODAY?

(CLICK!) ...WORST DAY OF FIGHTING SINCE—(CLICK!) ...ALLEGATIONS OF FRAUD—

(CLICK!) ...KIDNAPPING— (CLICK!) ...EXECUTION-STYLE SLAYING—

(CLICK!) ...BRUTAL MURDER OF A TOURIST—

(CLICK!) ...SENTENCED FOR MOLEST— (CLICK!) ...MALNUTRITION— (CLICK!)...(CLICK!) (CLICK!)

♪♪ I LOVE YOU, YOU LOVE ME, WE'RE A GREAT BIG FAM-I-LY... ♪

KIRKMAN & SCOTT

28

29

BABY BLUES
Rick Kirkman / Jerry Scott

DA-DA?

NO. DADDY'S AT WORK, ZOE.

DADDY WORKS IN A BIG OFFICE WHERE HE HAS A DESK AND A COMPUTER AND GETS TO TALK TO OTHER ADULTS ALL DAY LONG AND GO TO NICE RESTAURANTS FOR LUNCH WITH INTERESTING PEOPLE.

MOMMY HAD TO PUT **HER** CAREER ON HOLD WHILE SHE JUST SITS HERE WATCHING YOU GROW UP!

MA MA ♥

SMACK!

♥ POOR DADDY. ♥

KIRKMAN & SCOTT

We don't do a great deal of jokes about diapers, but once in a while, an idea is just too good to waste.

33

 COME IN HERE A MINUTE WHILE MOMMY TRIES ON THIS DRESS, OKAY, ZOE?

 DON'T PULL ON THAT, HONEY... MOMMY HAS TO TRY THAT ON.

 WAIT! DON'T TEAR THAT TAG! IT BELONGS TO THE STORE!

RIP!

 MOMMY WANTS TO SEE IF THIS DRESS LOOKS G—AAAGH! DON'T PUT THAT IN YOUR MOUTH! IT'S YUCKY!

 JUST SIT STILL ONE MORE MINUTE, ZOE, THEN WE CAN...

 ...GO.

MAMA!

 FIND ANY BARGAINS TODAY?

THEY HAD A SALE ON HUMILIATION.

Panel 1: BUTCH AND BUNNY WANT TO KNOW IF WE WANT STEAK OR CHICKEN?

WHAT??

Panel 2: OUR **PERFECT** NEIGHBORS WANT US TO COME TO THEIR **PERFECT** HOUSE WHILE THEY COOK **PERFECT** FOOD IN THEIR **PERFECT** BACK YARD, AND THEY WANT **US** TO CHOOSE THE MENU? **NO WAY!**

Panel 3: NO WAY DO I WANT TO BE RESPONSIBLE FOR RUINING THEIR **PERFECT** GET-TOGETHER!

Panel 4: STEAK. HOLD THE PERFECTION.

Butch and Bunny, a perfect couple who do everything better than Darryl and Wanda, moved in next door a few years into the strip. Every neighborhood must have a Butch and Bunny because the mail pours in every time they make an appearance.

Panel 5: I DON'T KNOW WHY WE'RE GOING TO THIS BARBECUE... BUTCH AND BUNNY DRIVE ME CRAZY!

Panel 6: WHY?

WHY?? BECAUSE THEY'RE SO PERFECT!

Panel 7: THEIR HOUSE IS PERFECT... THEIR BODIES ARE PERFECT... NAME ONE THING IN THEIR LIVES THAT ISN'T PERFECT!

KIRKMAN & SCOTT

Panel 8: THEIR NEXT-DOOR NEIGHBORS?

THANKS... I FEEL MUCH BETTER NOW.

Panel 9: I DON'T KNOW WHAT WE'RE DOING HERE... I CAN'T STAND BUNNY.

BING! BONG!

Panel 10: SHE ALWAYS ACTS SO PERKY... SO CHEERFUL... SO ENTHUSIASTIC...

Panel 11: HIIIII!

HIIIIII! GREAT TO SEE YOU!

KISS! KISS!

Panel 12: WHAT A PHONY.

KIRKMAN & SCOTT

35

Conflict is the essence of the humor in *Baby Blues*, so when we noticed that Darryl and Wanda were getting the hang of parenting Zoe, we knew something had to be done.

Wanda discovered that she was pregnant again in early 1994, and after a short fifteen-month pregnancy, gave birth to Hamish MacPherson on April 29, 1995. So far, nobody likes his name.

There's a difference between conflict and cruelty, and two kids in diapers at the same time is more than anyone should have to endure. So we had Darryl and Wanda start potty-training Zoe soon after Hammie was born.

DO YOU HAVE TO GO POTTY, ZOE?
UH-HUH.

CODE YELLOW!

OH, WELL— WE'LL JUST HAVE TO START MOVING FASTER.
UH-OH.

ARE YOU KIDDING? FIREFIGHTERS DON'T HAVE THIS KIND OF RESPONSE TIME!

OKAY ⟩GASP!⟨... THE BILLS ARE FINALLY PAID!

⟩GROAN!⟨ EIGHT LOADS OF LAUNDRY...WASHED, DRIED, FOLDED AND PUT AWAY!

I WISH YOU WOULDN'T MARTYR WHILE I'M MARTYRING.
HEY—I MARTYRED FIRST!

The great thing about cartoon characters is that they can blurt out stuff that we all think, but are too afraid (or too smart) to say.

THE HOUSE IS A WRECK, THE SINK IS FULL OF DIRTY DISHES, THE KIDS CRIED ALL DAY, MY HAIR IS A MESS...

AND I THINK I'M THE LUCKIEST GUY IN THE WORLD!

REALLY?

BECAUSE YOUR FAMILY IS SO IMPORTANT TO YOU?
BECAUSE I COMMUTE.

Baby Blues took a creative turn around mid-1995. Zoe was now able to walk and speak for herself, and started exercising her independence. Now Darryl and Wanda were not just befuddled by the demands of raising two children, they were befuddled by the demands of one who could talk back.

39

OH WOW... LOOK AT THAT POOR WOMAN!

TRYING TO GO SHOPPING WITH A COUPLE OF WILD KIDS!

THE POOR THING LOOKS SO **FRAZZLED!** SO **TIRED!** SO **EXHAUS**—

WAA-AAA!

HEY, WAIT A MINUTE!

2 DAY SALE

WHY DOES ZOE LIKE YOU SO MUCH?

I'M THE ONE WHO BATHES HER... **I'M** THE ONE WHO DRESSES HER ... **I'M** THE ONE WHO BRUSHES HER TEETH...**I'M** THE ONE WHO COMBS HER HAIR,... ALL **YOU** HAVE TO DO IS COME HOME AND PLAY WITH HER!

I GUESS THAT EXPLAINS IT, DOESN'T IT?

OH.

I WANT TO BE THE DAD FOR A WHILE!

Wanda had a tough time dealing with the trauma of Zoe's first immunizations, so she figured out an ingenious way to cope with Hammie's first shots . . . desertion.

HAM HAS HIS FIRST DOCTOR'S APPOINTMENT TOMORROW.

OOOH... SHOTS.

NOW, WANDA, I DON'T WANT YOU TO BE NERVOUS. WE BOTH KNOW THAT THE RISK FOR SERIOUS REACTION TO IMMUNIZATION IS VERY SMALL, RIGHT?

RIGHT.

SO I DON'T WANT YOU TO GET ALL FREAKED OUT LIKE YOU DID WHEN ZOE GOT HER SHOTS.

I WON'T...

...BECAUSE YOU'RE TAKING HIM BY YOURSELF.

WHAT??

I'M GOING TO BE STRAIGHT WITH YOU, SON... WE'RE ON OUR WAY TO THE DOCTOR, AND YOU'RE GOING TO GET SOME SHOTS.

IT'S NOT GOING TO BE FUN, BUT THERE'S NOTHING TO BE AFRAID OF.

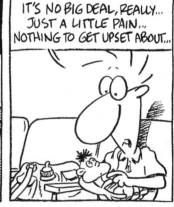

IT'S NO BIG DEAL, REALLY... JUST A LITTLE PAIN... NOTHING TO GET UPSET ABOUT...

HAMISH MacPHERSON?

HERE!

HEY, YOU'RE BACK! HOW DID IT GO?

¡GROAN! TERRIFIC.

TWO DIRTY DIAPERS, A THIRTY-MINUTE WAIT IN THE DOCTOR'S OFFICE, THREE SHOTS, A SCREAMING FIT YOU WOULDN'T BELIEVE, **AND** HE BARFED ON MY PANTS.

BOY, AM I GLAD THIS DAY IS OVER!

IT'S TEN-FIFTEEN IN THE MORNING.

This is one of the few strips we've done that deals directly with the main difference between changing a baby girl's and a baby boy's diapers.

Every once in a while, you get reminded of the toll parenting can take on your looks.

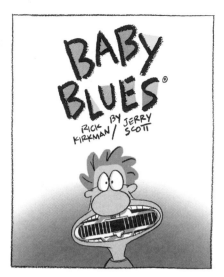

BABY BLUES

BY RICK KIRKMAN / JERRY SCOTT

...SO THEN BITSY ENDED UP EATING MITZY'S FOOD BY MISTAKE! YOU SHOULD'VE SEEN THE LOOK ON THAT LITTLE DOG'S FACE!

HAR! HAR! HAR! SNORT!

HEH.

SIGH!

WAAA-AA-AA-AA!

UH-OH... THE BABY IS CR—

I'LL GO!

WEH! WEH! WEH!

HEY THERE, BIG GUY! IT'S ALL RIGHT... DADDY'S HERE.

WHIMPER! WHIMPER!

SHHH...THERE'S NOTHING TO CRY ABOUT, AT LEAST YOU'RE IN HERE AND NOT OUT THERE WITH THE ARNETTES!

TALK ABOUT A COUPLE OF WINDBAGS! YAK, YAK, YAK... THEY HAVEN'T SHUT UP SINCE THEY GOT HERE!

AND WHAT DO THEY TALK ABOUT? **NOTHING!** FOR A WHILE THERE, I THOUGHT IT MIGHT ACTUALLY BE POSSIBLE TO **DIE** OF BOREDOM! YOU SAVED MY LIFE!

PLUS, HAVE YOU EVER REALLY **LOOKED** AT THE ARNETTES? HOW DO PEOPLE THAT WEIRD FIND EACHOTHER? I TELL YOU, IT'S —

—WHAT'S WRONG?

KIRKMAN & SCOTT

WHAT DO YOU **MEAN** THE BABY MONITOR IS STILL ON??

In October 1995, Wanda's dad, Hugh, suffered a heart attack. He's since recovered, lost thirty pounds, and maintains the cholesterol level of melba toast, but this was Wanda's first brush with mortality.

Being a cartoonist is not as physically demanding as one might suspect, so we're always complaining about wanting to lose weight. This strip must have run around the time one or both of us was trying to get in shape. Not everything that happens to us makes it into the strip . . . just the embarrassing stuff.

48

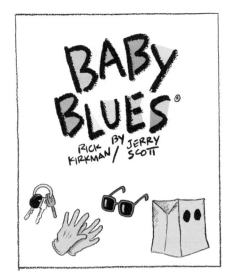

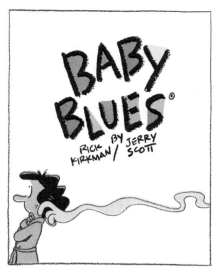

BABY BLUES®
BY RICK KIRKMAN / JERRY SCOTT

DOES THIS ROOM SMELL FUNNY TO YOU?

FUNNY "HA-HA," OR FUNNY "EWWWW"?

FUNNY "EWWW."

NOW THAT YOU MENTION IT, SNIFF! SNIFF! YEAH... IT DOES.

WHAT COULD IT BE?

I THINK IT'S COMING FROM OVER THERE.

SNIFF! SNIFF! SNIFF!

SNIFF! SNIFF! SNIFF!

AHA! **THAT'S** WHAT IT IS!

ZOE'S SIPPY CUP MUST HAVE ROLLED UNDER HERE, AND THE MILK WENT SOUR... GROSS!

I FOUND IT!

UH-OH...

UH-OH...

KIRKMAN & SCOTT

Kids are such givers. Between us, ours have given us 8,963 colds.

TICKLE! TICKLE! TICKLE!

DADDY!

HI, ZOE! TELL ME ABOUT YOUR DAY!

HAMMIE BARFED!

AM I GLAD TO BE HOME! MY STUPID COMPUTER WAS GIVING ME TROUBLE ALL DAY!

IT MADE ALL KINDS OF NOISE, THEN IT JUST SAT THERE BLINKING AT ME, NOT DOING ANYTHING I WANTED IT TO... AND THEN IT CRASHED!

I DON'T GET IT... THE THING IS ONLY A COUPLE OF YEARS OLD!

WELL, THERE'S YOUR PROBLEM RIGHT THERE.

WHAT?

YOUR COMPUTER IS A TODDLER.

SIGH!

WHAT'S WRONG, HONEY?

I DON'T KNOW...IT'S JUST THAT.. SOMETIMES I FEEL SO...I JUST WISH I HAD SOME TIME TO... OH, NEVER MIND.

COME ON... GET IT OFF YOUR CHEST.

I CAN'T, IT'S ATTACHED.

TEA, DADDY?

WHY, THANK YOU, SWEETHEART! HOW NICE!

MMMM! DELICIOUS! MAY I HAVE SECONDS, PLEASE?

SURE! I GO GET S'MORE!

One of the first lessons to be learned as the parent of a toddler is to always question the origin of food or drink offered to you by the child. And even if it seems okay, it's still a good idea not to eat or drink it.

Darryl and Wanda have so fine-tuned their communication over the years that messages can be delivered without speaking at all.

This is more of a home movie than a comic strip.

Breast-feeding has been an important part of the background in *Baby Blues* from the beginning. It's not a subject we generally focus on, but once in a while we find reason to bring attention to the issue. A newspaper article about a woman who was outrageously expelled from a public swimming pool for breast-feeding in public sparked this series.

We had heard that some kids prefer to roll around instead of crawling. It seemed like a very weird image, therefore perfect for *Baby Blues*. We received an astonishing number of letters from readers whose kids also rolled. Go figure.

Hillary Clinton sent us a personal letter about this strip. Apparently it's one of the few instances where her book was mentioned without being blasted. She said the original is hanging in the White House.

BABY BLUES
BY JERRY SCOTT / RICK KIRKMAN

HONEY, WOULD YOU PUT THAT LOAD OF CLOTHES IN THE WASHING MACHINE FOR ME?

SURE.

SMALL, MEDIUM OR LARGE LOAD?

LARGE.

HOT, WARM OR COLD WATER?

WARM.

BLEACH OR NO BLEACH?

NO BLEACH!

LEVEL CUP OR HEAPING CUP OF DETERGENT?

I DON'T KNOW... LEVEL! IT DOESN'T MATTER!

SHOULD THE SOAP GO IN **UNDER** THE CLOTHES, OR ON **TOP** OF THE CLOTHES?

I DON'T CARE! JUST TURN THE STUPID THING ON!!!

SLOSH! SLOSH!

ANYTHING ELSE I CAN DO TO HELP OUT, HONEY?

Baby Blues® From Conception to Delivery

Jerry: It all starts with the writing. Like a movie, a TV show, or a play, a script must be written first. I start with broad ideas, punch lines, funny words, and little sketches scribbled out longhand on a pad of paper. It's an exhilarating process that involves sitting in one spot and daydreaming for up to three days straight (don't try this at home. . . I'm a professional). I prefer to work in batches of six or twelve strips at a time, so when that many promising scribbles appear on my tablet (or when our editor starts screaming), I sit down at the computer and begin to work out the staging, timing, and dialogue. Each panel is numbered and starts with a description of the scene, the characters involved, their mood, their activity, and the dialogue. Sometimes my direction is very specific, but more often I leave room for Rick to interpret the joke as he sees fit and adjust the staging to his liking. After I'm satisfied with the batch of gags, I E-mail them to Rick.

Rick: When I receive the gags from Jerry, the first thing I do is to look for key descriptive phrases like "room full of laundry," "crowded mall/stadium," or "floor covered with toys." I conveniently misplace those right off the bat. Then I look for the gags that strike me as the funniest and I start drawing. I first do the pencil sketch on tracing paper that I've preruled with the border outlines of the panels.

This is the most fun and challenging stage of the process. Problem solving is just as important as the art. I can also be a little more loose and spontaneous with the drawings. The dialogue for the whole strip is penciled first so I will know how much room I have for the characters. I may have to adjust the wording of a gag in order to make it fit better. In some cases, I may have a suggestion for the dialogue, in which case I either make it in the balloon, or give Jerry an alternate in the margin.

I usually have a good bit of the strip already visualized ahead of time, so it's just a matter of putting it to paper. Other times I may struggle with it, cutting and taping bits and pieces of drawings together. Once drawn, I fax copies of the rough sketches to Jerry.

Jerry: Despite the look on my face in this picture, this is my favorite part of the process. After I receive the faxes, I sit down and try to read them as if I've never seen them before. It's really fun because Rick often makes changes in the action and dialogue; many of the strips look completely different (and usually better) than I had envisioned them. Plus, there's something cool about the loose pencil sketchiness and spontaneity of a comic strip rough. After making my notes, I call Rick and we talk through the strips, looking for opportunities to make each one better. Strangely enough, after ten years of this, we still haven't strangled each other to death.

Rick: It's time to finish the art. For those of you interested in the nuts and bolts: the dailies are drawn on a Starwhite Vicksburg cover stock that's been preprinted with nonphoto blue borders, and the Sundays are on Strathmore 100 percent cotton, two-ply kid-finish bristol board. I use either Berol Prismacolor or the Faber-Castell Polychromos black colored pencils. I place the board over a copy of the sketch and, on the light box, trace everything

a little more deliberately than I drew it the first time. I do try to retain some of the original spontaneity by not adhering too strictly to the sketch.

When the main drawing is finished, I draw in the border lines freehand and add the copyright lines and signature. Mistakes are corrected with an electric eraser and Pro White paint. Now that the strips are finished, I put on the dates, photocopy them onto laser paper, and FedEx them to the syndicate.

This is the most exhilarating part of the process. All the suspense and drama that one could possibly want in their life can be found in my trips to FedEx. After a brief sigh of relief, it's time to start all over again.

Sunday strips are done in this same basic process, except that the color work is done here on a Macintosh computer using Adobe Photoshop. After coloring the strip on the computer, the files are uploaded via the Internet to appear in the newspaper about six weeks later.

Rick and his new assistant.

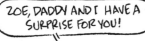

Being a parent makes you a better salesperson.

ARE YOU SURE YOU HAVE TO LEAVE ALREADY?

YES...WE PROMISED AUNT MIN A VISIT, AND IT'S A TWO-HOUR DRIVE.

SHE BROKE HER HIP, YOU KNOW, AND HASN'T BEEN GETTING AROUND VERY WELL. NOW, IF SHE LISTENED TO HER DOCTOR SHE WOULD BE MUCH BETTER OFF, BUT YOU KNOW AUNT MIN. OF COURSE, THE DOCTORS ALL LOOK LIKE KIDS TODAY, SO WHO CAN BLAME HER? I REMEMBER WHEN I HAD MY HYSTERECTOMY...

COME ON, MOTHER! IT'S LATE!

DADDY'S RIGHT. WE'D BETTER GET GOING IF WE PLAN ON GETTING OUT OF THERE BEFORE DARK.

YOU KNOW HOW AUNT MIN IS... TALK, TALK, TALK...

KIRKMAN & SCOTT

WHACK!
OW!

OH, GREAT.

HEY, WANDA... COME HERE FOR A MINUTE.

WHICH GOES BETTER WITH A BLUE SUIT... THE SESAME STREET BANDAGE OR THE SNOOPY?

GO WITH THE SNOOPY... IT BRINGS OUT THE COLOR IN YOUR EYES.

KIRKMAN & SCOTT

Years later, this is still happening to me: I was in a car dealership today when a salesperson commented about my thumb, "I *love* your bandage!" It was my kids'.
—R.K.

IS THAT ALL OF THEM?

YEP. THAT'S IT.

YESSS!! I KNEW IT!

WHAT??

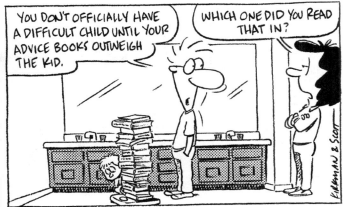
YOU DON'T OFFICIALLY HAVE A DIFFICULT CHILD UNTIL YOUR ADVICE BOOKS OUTWEIGH THE KID.

WHICH ONE DID YOU READ THAT IN?

KIRKMAN & SCOTT

Wanda is a stay-at-home mom by choice, but that doesn't stop her from being ambivalent about it, and maybe a little resentful at times. Even Darryl's mundane job sounds thrilling to Wanda after years of diapers, Play-Doh, and Barney.

One of the great joys in Zoe's life is being a major influence on Hammie.

DID YOU HEAR SOMETHING?

LIKE WHAT?

THERE WAS A SOFT "THUMP," THEN A BUNCH OF TINY "PIT-PATS," FOLLOWED BY A "CLANK" THAT SOUNDED LIKE THE COOKIE JAR LID, MORE "PIT-PATS," AND A SOFT "CRUNCH" SOUND.

YOU DIDN'T HEAR THAT...

NO.

I THINK YOU'RE IMAGINING THINGS.

ME TOO. TURN IT UP.

KIRKMAN & SCOTT

EAT YOUR PEAS.

I DON'T WIKE PEAS.

SURE YOU DO! YOU'VE ALWAYS LIKED PEAS! PEAS ARE YOUR FAVORITE VEGETABLE, REMEMBER?

OH YEAH... I FORGOT. I DO WIKE PEAS!

I JUST DON'T WIKE THESE PEAS.

YOUR TURN.

IS THERE ANYTHING I CAN DO TO HELP YOU, HONEY?

NO, DEAR. YOU'VE HAD A HARD DAY...

WHY DON'T YOU JUST GO IN THE LIVING ROOM AND PUT YOUR FEET UP WHILE I FINISH THE DISHES, GET THE KIDS READY FOR BED, CLEAN UP THE LIVING ROOM, DO A COUPLE OF LOADS OF LAUNDRY, AND WASH THE CAR.

WELL... OKAY! THANKS!

YOU'D THINK AFTER THIS MANY YEARS OF MARRIAGE, I'D BE ABLE TO RECOGNIZE SARCASM.

KIRKMAN & SCOTT

71

EAT SOME MORE CHICKEN, ZOE.

WHAT?

EAT SOME MORE OF YOUR CHICKEN.

WHAT?

YOUR CHICKEN! THE LIGHT BROWN STUFF! PLEASE PUT SOME OF IT ON YOUR FORK, PUT THE FORK IN YOUR MOUTH, THEN CHEW AND SWALLOW!

WHEN?

TAP TAP TAP!

WOW! AND ALL MY LIFE I THOUGHT THAT ONLY HAPPENED IN CARTOONS!

REMEMBER A COUPLE OF YEARS AGO WHEN OUR CHRISTMAS CARDS WENT OUT LATE, SO WE WROTE "HAPPY HOLIDAYS" INSTEAD OF "MERRY CHRISTMAS" INSIDE?

YEP.

AND THEN THE NEXT YEAR WE WERE EVEN LATER, SO "HAPPY HOLIDAYS" BECAME "SEASON'S GREETINGS"?

HA! YEAH.

ANY IDEAS FOR THIS YEAR?

HOW ABOUT "HAPPY EASTER"?

IT'S DECEMBER 24th, ZOE!

REALLY?!

TONIGHT IS THE NIGHT THAT EIGHT REINDEER AND RUDOLPH WILL LAND ON OUR ROOF, AND SANTA CLAUS WILL SLIDE DOWN OUR CHIMNEY WITH A BIG BAG OF TOYS FOR YOU!

WOW!!

TOMORROW MORNING THERE WILL BE LOTS OF PRESENTS AND CANDY UNDER THE CHRISTMAS TREE FOR YOU AND HAMMIE TO OPEN!

YAY!!!

OH BOY! TOYS! OH BOY! TOYS! OH BOY! TOYS!

THE MEDIA SHOULD BE ASHAMED FOR TURNING THIS INTO SUCH A COMMERCIAL HOLIDAY.

When our daughter was born, we vowed to raise her with unisex toys so that she would have a better sense of herself as a whole person and not just as a "pretty little girl." At last count, there are seventeen Barbie dolls in her room and the only color she'll wear in public is pink. —J.S.

BABY BLUES®
BY RICK KIRKMAN / JERRY SCOTT

WHAT DO YOU THINK?

I DON'T KNOW... IT'S UP TO YOU.

WELL, IF WE WAIT UNTIL NEW YEAR'S TO TAKE THE CHRISTMAS TREE DOWN, THE NEEDLES ARE GOING TO START FALLING OFF AND MAKE A HUGE MESS IN HERE.

OKAY.

REMEMBER LAST YEAR? I WAS STILL VACUUMING UP PINE NEEDLES AT EASTER!

UH-HUH.

PLUS, WE WON'T FEEL LIKE DOING IT ON THE FIRST BECAUSE WE'RE GOING OUT WITH RHONDA ON NEW YEAR'S EVE.

GOOD POINT.

BESIDES, THESE THINGS BECOME A REAL FIRE HAZARD WHEN THEY DRY OUT!

YEP.

I SAW A REPORT ON THE NEWS WHERE THEY PUT A MATCH TO A DRY TREE LIKE THIS, AND IT BURNED IN THREE SECONDS!

I KNOW.

WHAT A RELIEF TO HAVE THAT OUT OF THE WAY! NOW WE DON'T HAVE TO WORRY ABOUT IT ANY MORE.

HEY! WHERE'S DA KWISMUS TWEE?!

I HOPE YOU'RE HAPPY.

KIRKMAN & SCOTT

75

DO YOU THINK I SHOULD WEAR THIS LONG DRESS OR THE LITTLE BLACK ONE?

THEY'RE BOTH KIND OF DRESSY, AREN'T THEY?

NOT FOR A NEW YEAR'S EVE PARTY... RHONDA SAID IT'S BLACK TIE, REMEMBER?

DO I REALLY **HAVE** TO WEAR THE TUX?

YES, YOU **HAVE** TO WEAR THE TUX... **AND** THE TIE... **AND** GOOD SHOES... **AND** THE CUMMERBUND. ANY OTHER QUESTIONS?

DO WE HAVE TO STAY OUT LATE?

MY FIRST CHANCE IN AGES TO GREET BABY NEW YEAR, AND MY DATE IS FATHER TIME.

KIRKMAN & SCOTT

WE'RE LEAVING NOW. I WANT YOU TO PROMISE ME THAT YOU'LL BE GOOD TONIGHT.

THAT MEANS NO WHINING, NO POUTING, NO COMPLAINING, AND NO TANTRUMS... GOT THAT?

KIRKMAN & SCOTT

AND THAT GOES FOR YOU GUYS, TOO.

WAS THAT A GREAT NEW YEAR'S PARTY, OR WHAT?

OH YEAH.

WHAT A CROWD! WHAT A BAND! WHAT AN EVENING!

PRETTY WILD ALL RIGHT.

WELL. I DON'T KNOW ABOUT YOU, BUT I HAD A BLAST!

I COULD TELL...

ARE YOU SAYING I MADE A FOOL OF MYSELF?

I'M SAYING THAT DOING THE MACARENA TO "AULD LANG SYNE" WAS PUSHING IT.

KIRKMAN & SCOTT

1. DEAR AUNT RHONDA...

YEAH... DAT'S GOOD.

2. THANK YOU FOR THE GREAT CHRISTMAS PRESENT.

UH-HUH.

DID YOU MENTION YOU TOLD ZOE THAT BARBIE® IS A FREAK OF NATURE, NOT THE STANDARD OF BEAUTY?

IS THAT REALLY RELEVANT?

AIEEEEEE

IT'S BARBIE®!! RUN, TEDDY! RUN!!

3. IT IS MY VERY FIRST BARBIE® DOLL, AND I PLAY WITH IT EVERY DAY. LOVE, ZOE

4. DOES THAT SOUND OKAY?

YEP! BYE!

KIRKMAN & SCOTT

We try to raise the disaster stakes every time Zoe has a birthday party.

79

This is one of those "day in the life" strips. This happened almost panel-for-panel to me one morning a year or so ago. I'm thinking of switching to boxer shorts. —J.S.

Baby Blues

by Rick Kirkman / Jerry Scott

TAKE MY BRUDDER...

...PLEASE.

WHAT A CUTE LITTLE BROTHER YOU HAVE! WHAT'S HIS NAME?

Linens

DOO-DOO-HEAD.

ZOE!

I THINK YOU MUST BE KIDDING ME... WHAT'S HIS REAL NAME?

DOO-DOO HEAD!

ZOE! YOU KNOW BETTER THAN THAT!

YOU STRAIGHTEN UP AND TELL THE NICE LADY YOUR BROTHER'S NAME!

OKA-A-A-Y...

NOW, WHAT'S HIS NAME, REALLY?

HAMMIE.

FINE! IF YOU DON'T WANT TO TELL ME, DON'T TELL ME!

NO! REALLY! THAT'S HIS NAME!

AN' HE DOESN'T CRAWL... HE ROLLS!

KIRKMAN & SCOTT

Linda knows that [breast]feeding is important, [she] still feels a little trapped at times.

HEY THERE, LITTLE BUDDY! NEED A LIFT?

I HOPE YOU LEARN TO CRAWL ONE OF THESE DAYS... YOU'LL NEVER GET VERY FAR BY ROLLING.

There are times that when I need an idea all I have to do is go up to the house and wait a few minutes. One day I happened to be standing in the laundry room. —J.S.

89

I'M THE DOCTOR AN' YOU'RE THE SICK PERSON, OKAY, DADDY?

OKAY DOC.

OOOOOHHH! AAARGH! I NEED A DOCTOR!

OKAY JUSTA MINUTE.

FIRST, I TAKE YOUR TEMPERATURE...

OW!

JAB

...THEN I LOOK IN YOUR EARS...

HEY!

NOW WHERE'S MY OTHER STUFF?

BOOF!

SAY AAAAHH...

AAACCCK!

GOTTA GO.... AMB'LANCE IS COMING!

AAGH! OOOCH! OWW!

WHAT'S WRONG WITH YOU?

I NEED A NEW HEALTH PLAN.

KIRKMAN & SCOTT

It seems like the level of drama in our house increases with each new Disney animated feature that's released. —J.S.

ZOE MADE DARRYL THE CUTEST VALENTINE'S CARD...

LET ME SEE.

SHE GLUED ON THE SEQUINS AND PIPE CLEANERS AND PAINTED IT ALL BY HERSELF.

HOW SWEET!

"Roses are red,
Violets are sad.
Take Mommy to dinner,
She needs it real bad."

I HELPED WITH THE WORDING.

YOU CAN'T REALLY TELL.

≥AHEM!≤

OOOH! CANDY AND FLOWERS! HOW SWEET!

AND THAT'S NOT ALL...

TA-DAAAH!

≥GASP!≤ OH, DARRYL! JUST WHAT I WANTED...

...A REAL BABY-SITTER!

IT'S JUST A RENTAL... GO GET DRESSED.

HAPPY VALENTINE'S DAY, MRS. MacPHERSON.

THWACK!

TRIP! Thunk! SCRAPE!

BONK!

I THINK WE'D BETTER POSTPONE ZOE'S CHECKUP.

YEAH... SHE LOOKS TOO MUCH LIKE SHE NEEDS TO SEE A DOCTOR TO GO SEE THE DOCTOR.

It's always reason for celebration when your kids grow out of their obligationwear.

95

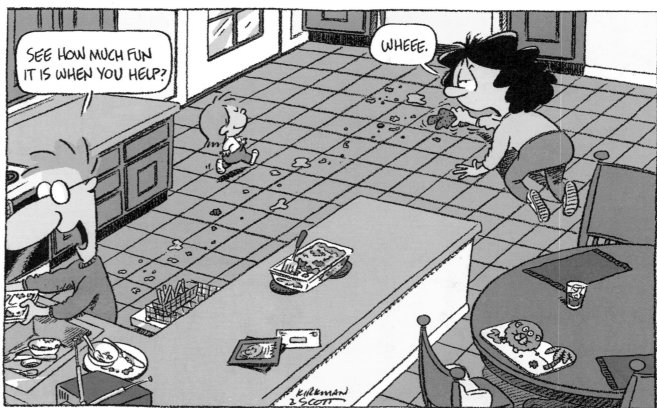

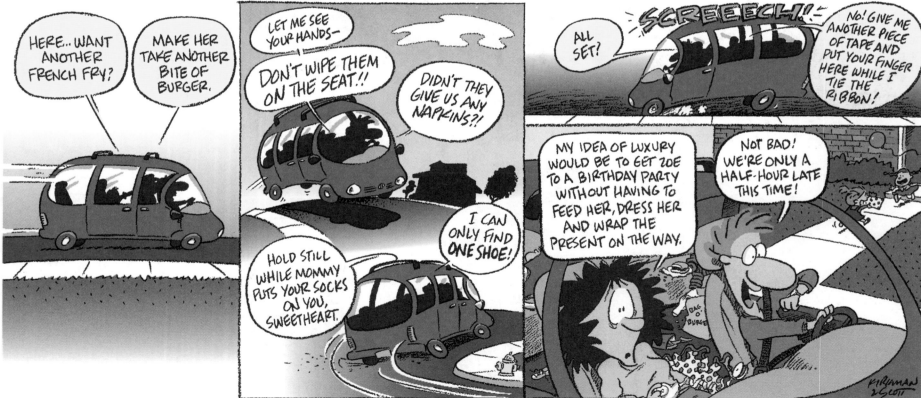

Possibly the first syndicated comic strip in history to use the word "nipple." We're very proud.

WHERE WOULD I FIND THE MEASURING SPOONS?

PROBABLY THE SAME PLACE YOU'D FIND ALL THE OTHER KITCHEN UTENSILS.

OH YEAH. WHAT WAS I THINKING?

DO YOU NEED ANYTHING WHILE I'M OUT HERE?

Potty-training makes you do things only another parent would understand.

101

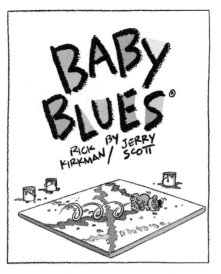

Darryl, like most of us daddies, is a total sucker.

My daughter started telling me made-up knock-knock jokes a couple of years ago, and they still don't make any sense. —J.S.

My wife, Sukey, actually caught herself saying this one day. Of course, I was helpful with the situation, as always, when I said, "Wait! Let me write that down!" —R.K.

A lot of our friends and family have children that are either in or almost ready for college. This strip is just a visit from the Ghost of Tuition To Come for us.

108

This one makes me cringe—reminding me of the time when our four-year-old daughter dislocated my wrist . . . but that's another story. Ouch. —R.K.

The idea for this strip came unsolicited from a reader. These home-made ideas rarely work, but this one was so purely surprising and funny that we just couldn't resist.

SLAM!

I THINK I'LL GO CLEAN THE GUTTERS, HOSE DOWN THE DRIVEWAY, AND WASH THE CARS.

WOW! THAT'S PRETTY AMBITIOUS!

IT'S EITHER THAT OR MATCH UP A DRYERFUL OF BABY SOCKS.

HEY! WAIT A MINUTE!

ON SECOND THOUGHT, MAYBE HAMMIE COULD SKIP HIS NAP TODAY...

WIMP.

RING!

HELLO? HELLO?

RING!

HELLO? HELLO? HELLOOOO!!!

RING! RING!

YOU HAVE TO PICK IT UP FIRST.

OH.

RING!

111

Another new wrinkle for the MacPhersons came about once Zoe was old enough for preschool.

DARRYL! GUESS WHAT?... I FOUND THE **PERFECT** PRESCHOOL FOR ZOE.

IT'S CLOSE-BY, THEY HAVE A CLASS FOR THREE-YEAR-OLDS, GREAT TEACHERS, AND SHE CAN START NEXT WEEK!

THERE'S ONLY ONE PROBLEM. IT'S THE BEST PRESCHOOL IN THE CITY, AND THEY THINK ZOE HAS THE PERFECT QUALIFICATIONS.

SO WHAT'S THE PROBLEM?

THEY'RE NOT SURE **WE** DO.

MR. AND MRS. MacPHERSON, I'M GEOFFREY ENGLE, THE HEADMASTER HERE AT REDFIELD PRESCHOOL.

REDFIELD IS THE FINEST PRE-SCHOOL IN THE STATE, WINNER OF THE PRESTIGIOUS "EDUCA-TOR'S TROPHY" THREE YEARS RUNNING, AND THIS YEAR'S RECIPIENT OF THE COVETED "PLATINUM CRAYON AWARD."

MY!

WOW!

NOW, HOW MAY I HELP YOU?

WE'D LIKE TO ENROLL OUR DAUGHTER HERE.

WONDERFUL! WHEN WILL SHE BE BORN?

I SMELL **WAITING LIST.**

WELL, WE FOUND A REALLY GOOD PRESCHOOL FOR ZOE TODAY.

HEY, THAT'S GREAT!

MY SCHOOL!

SHE STARTS NEXT WEEK: TUESDAYS AND THURSDAYS, NINE TO ELEVEN-THIRTY.

TERRIFIC!

SCHOOL! SCHOOL! SCHOOL!

GREAT!

EXCITING!

YOU BET!

WONDERFUL!

A MILESTONE!

YESSIREE!

WAAAAAA!

My daughter's first haircut, accurate down to the hairdresser's real name (Hi, Rachela!). —J.S.

WAAAAAAAAAAAAA! WAAAAAAAAA! WAAAAAAAAAAAAAAAAAAAA! WAAAAAAAAAA!

117

Occasionally, as a charity donation, we offer the chance for people to have their child's name appear in *Baby Blues*. This is one of those strips. Lucky Trent . . . the first kid in history to give chicken pox to a comic strip character.

CHINKITTY-CLINK!
CHINKITTY-CLINK!
CHINKITTY-CLINK!

WHAT THE-?

OH GOOD! YOU'RE HOME! DINNER IS IN THE OVEN...WE'LL BE BACK BY EIGHT O'CLOCK.

DADDY!

THE VAN IS MAKING A RATTLE BUT I DON'T THINK IT'S SERIOUS.

OKAY... BYE!

WAA-WAAAAA!

MO-O-MMY! HAMMIE TOUCHED ME!!

WHAT RATTLE?

119

THANKS AGAIN FOR A REALLY TERRIFIC MOTHER'S DAY, HONEY.

THE KIDS REALLY SEEMED TO ENJOY THEMSELVES.

THE ZOO... THE PARK... KIDDIELAND... THE ICE CREAM SHOP... WHAT A DAY!

ANYWAY, I WANTED YOU TO KNOW THAT I APPRECIATED ALL OF IT, AND I WON'T FORGET THIS MOTHER'S DAY FOR A LONG TIME.

YEAH, WELL **NEXT** TIME YOU'RE COMING **WITH** US YOU HEAR?

121

DO YOU EVER WONDER IF WE'RE PROVIDING THE KIDS WITH A GOOD CHILDHOOD?

LET'S SEE...THEIR OWN ROOMS, GOBS OF TOYS, STACKS OF BOOKS AND VIDEOS, ACCESS TO A COLOR TV AND A VCR, A PRIVATE BATHROOM, RECREATIONAL ACTIVITIES, A CAR AND DRIVER TO TAKE THEM ANYWHERE THEY NEED TO GO...

THIS ISN'T CHILDHOOD... IT'S A RESORT!

KIRKMAN & SCOTT

This strip got us in trouble. My mom told me that mothers used to let their kids play with other kids who had chicken pox so they could catch it and get it over with. It struck me as funny, so Wanda and Yolanda hatched the same scheme. We heard from *lots* of moms and doctors who educated us about the dangers of this, and we made Wanda promise not to do it again. —J.S.

YOLANDA? IT'S WANDA.

I DON'T THINK YOU WANT KEESHA TO COME OVER TODAY...ZOE HAS CHICKENPOX.

KNOCK! KNOCK! KNOCK!

HANG ON... SOMEBODY IS AT THE DOOR.

YOLANDA...

COUGH UP SOME GERMS! WE WANT TO GET IT OVER WITH.

KIRKMAN & SCOTT

HI, HONEY... HOW ARE THE KIDS DOING?

JUST PEACHY.

THEIR CHICKENPOX IS ITCHING LIKE CRAZY, THEY'RE BORED, AND THE VCR JUST STOPPED WORKING.

POOR LITTLE KIDS...

IS THERE ANYTHING THAT I CAN PICK UP ON THE WAY HOME THAT WOULD HELP?

A QUART OF RUM AND TWO TICKETS TO HAWAII.

I MEANT FOR THE KIDS.

KIRKMAN & SCOTT

122

...I READ SOMEWHERE THAT IF YOU FASTEN THE BRACKET—
DADDY! DADDY! DADDY!

ZOE, DADDY IS ON THE PHONE! IT'S NOT POLITE TO INTERRUPT.
OH.

ANYWAY, IF YOU FASTEN THE BRACKET TO THE—
DADDY! DADDY! DADDY!

WHAT DOES "INTERRUPT" MEAN?

WAKE UP, ZOE! HURRY! WE HAVE TO GET READY FOR PRESCHOOL!
ZZZZ.

EAT! GIVE ME YOUR FOOT! POINT YOUR TOES! CHEW! SWALLOW!

TUCK YOUR SHIRT IN! DON'T RUN! BE CAREFUL! HAVE FUN! I LOVE YOU!

I USED TO THINK I WAS BUSY... THEN I BECAME THE MOTHER OF A PRESCHOOLER!
ROOKIE, EH?

I'M THE DOCTOR AN' YOU BE THE SICK GUY.
OKAY.

SAY "AHH."
AHHHHHHH...

AHHHHHH—
ZOE! HOW MANY TIMES HAVE I TOLD YOU TO STOP TAKING THAT FILTHY STICK OUT OF THE TRASH??

AHHHHHHHHHHH...

This is an addendum to the rule stated earlier about always questioning the origin of food offered by a toddler: Always avoid anything a toddler tries to put in or near your mouth.

125

28 June 1997

I am a graduate student at North Carolina State University studying honey bees and would like to ask for permission for myself and another student to reproduce the "bee barf" comic, in whole or in part, in a popular article we are writing for a journal that deals with bee-related research. Our premise: Many people, some beekeepers included, do refer to honey as bee barf. Yet it isn't really barf; there is either no or a negligible amount of sugar digestion while

the flower nectar is inside the bee en route back to the hive. The nectar is stored in a special organ located before the actual bee stomach. All the chemical changes take place once the nectar has been stored and manipulated by other bees in the colony. However, "bee barf" is a term we run across fairly frequently, from the general public and beekeepers alike. And we feel that since there is a sizeable number of people that may take "bee barf" literally, a little article explaining the actual process of nectar-to-honey is in order.

GNAW! GNAW! GNAW! GNAW!

DO YOU HEAR SOMETHING?

YEAH.

GNAW! GNAW! GNAW! GNAW!

IT SOUNDS LIKE CHEWING OR SOMETHING.

YOU DON'T SUPPOSE IT'S TERMITES, DO YOU?

GNAW! GNAW! GNAW! GNAW!

I DON'T KNOW... I'M NOT SURE WHERE IT'S—

—COMING FROM.

HEY! HAMMIE HAS ANOTHER TOOTH!

KIRKMAN & SCOTT

MOMMY!

HI, ZOE!

HOW WAS PRESCHOOL TODAY?

I DUNNO.

WELL, WHAT DID YOU **DO**?

I DUNNO.

DID YOU HEAR STORIES?

I DUNNO.

DID YOU DRAW PICTURES?

I DUNNO.

DID YOU PLAY ON THE SLIDE?

I DUNNO.

PRESCHOOL CAUSES AMNESIA.

HANDS SCHOOL

KIRKMAN & SCOTT

BOOGERNOSE!

ZOE!

WE DON'T USE LANGUAGE LIKE THAT AROUND HERE.

OH.

I WANT YOU TO TELL HAMMIE YOU'RE SORRY, AND PROMISE ME YOU'LL NEVER USE THAT WORD AGAIN.

I'M SORRY, I PROMISE.

HONESTLY! I DON'T KNOW WHERE SHE PICKS UP ALL THAT STUFF!

HIYA, BOOGERNOSE!

KIRKMAN & SCOTT

Uh . . . this one is straight out of my life. Being a good role model is hard. —J.S.

BPTH MNGL.

HAMMIE WANTS HIS TEDDY BEAR.

OKAY...

ONGL NFIG.

HAMMIE SAYS HE WOULD LIKE THAT TRUCK, TOO.

WOW! YOU REALLY UNDERSTAND HIM?

MMPTH GMM MAA!

HAMMIE SAYS HE WANTS HIS PACIFIER.

A TRANSLATOR! THIS IS GREAT!

MERPP.

AN' HE THINKS YOU SHOULD GIVE ME FIVE COOKIES.

NICE TRY.

BEFORE CHILDREN...

HOW CAN PEOPLE LET THEIR KIDS GO OUT DRESSED LIKE THAT?

YEAH.

AFTER CHILDREN...

WELL, AT LEAST SHE'S COVERED...

YEAH.

HOLD IT RIGHT THERE!

I JUST FINISHED CLEANING THE LIVING ROOM.

I DON'T EVER WANT TO HAVE TO CLEAN UP THE KIND OF MESS THAT WAS IN HERE AGAIN. UNDERSTAND?

YES.

HI, ZOE, WHAT'S NEW?

MOMMY SAID FROM NOW ON YOU HAVE TO CLEAN THE LIVING ROOM.

We goofed here. What we meant to say was, "The Difference Between First-Born and Second-Born Children." Of course, readers corrected us.

Kids learn a lot in school, but much of the real education happens on the playground.

Once we had children, the nature program became a viewing staple. We couldn't resist this set-up from the nature show. —R.K.

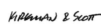
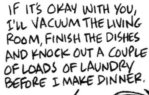

It's difficult to illustrate baby flatulence in a tasteful manner, but I think we accomplished it here. Probably another first for the comics pages. —J.S.

139

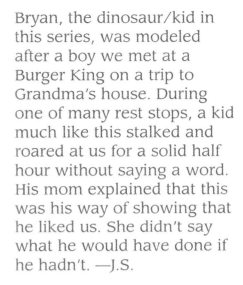

Bryan, the dinosaur/kid in this series, was modeled after a boy we met at a Burger King on a trip to Grandma's house. During one of many rest stops, a kid much like this stalked and roared at us for a solid half hour without saying a word. His mom explained that this was his way of showing that he liked us. She didn't say what he would have done if he hadn't. —J.S.

Mother Nature strikes again. Promoted as the story of a cute cuddly family of Meerkats, we were at first sucked in, until it turned into a Meerkat Massacre. Judging from our mail, we weren't the only ones traumatized by it. —R.K.

Dear Baby Blues cartoonists,

I totally agree that these nature shows on television push "realism" too far. Whatever happened to enjoying a family nature program minus meerkats-made-into-meatloaf?

Dear Baby Blues cartoonists,

You guys nailed it on "A Meerkat Family Saga." I taped it to watch with my seven-year-old nephew. The narrator's grandmotherly voice disarmed me and relaxed me such that every violent death was a shock. I am still disturbed by this "family" program. The producers should be working Psy-ops for the CIA. Thanks for a great strip.

Dear Baby Blues cartoonists,

Thank you . . . thank you . . . for the meerkat cartoons. I let out a huge hoot in the cafeteria when I read that.

Sometimes just a funny little doodle turns into a strip. *Beetle Bailey* cartoonist Mort Walker has this original strip in his collection.

ZOE, POLITE CHILDREN EAT WITH THEIR SPOONS AND FORKS.

THEY MUST NOT BE VERY HUNGRY!

SIGH!

WHAT'S WRONG, HONEY?

I PROMISED MYSELF THAT I WOULDN'T MAKE THE SAME MISTAKES WITH HAMMIE THAT I MADE WITH ZOE...

...AND FOR THE MOST PART, I HAVEN'T.

SO WHAT'S THE PROBLEM?

SIGH! I'M MAKING ALL **NEW** ONES.

WHINE! WHINE! WHINE!

WHINE! WHINE! WHINE!

ZOE, IF YOU DON'T STOP WHINING, I'LL GIVE YOU SOMETHING TO WHINE ABOUT!

HUH??

IT DOESN'T MAKE ANY SENSE TO ME, EITHER, BUT IT WORKED WHEN MY MOM USED TO SAY IT.

145

HAVE YOU NOTICED THAT WE DON'T CARRY AROUND AS MUCH STUFF FOR HAMMIE AS WE DID WITH ZOE?

NOW THAT YOU MENTION IT, THE DIAPER BAG DOES SEEM A LITTLE LIGHTER THAN IT USED TO.

IT'S WEIRD BECAUSE IT'S ALL THE SAME STUFF... DIAPERS... WIPES.... EXTRA CLOTHES— OH, WAIT! I KNOW WHAT'S MISSING!

WHAT?

THE ANXIETY.

YEAH, I GUESS THERE'S ALWAYS LESS OF THAT WITH THE SECOND BABY...

MOM! HAMMIE IS CRYING!

WANDA, HAVE YOU SEEN MY BELT?

MOM! HAMMIE BARFED!

I'M TAKING SOME OF YOUR CASH FOR LUNCH MONEY!

MOM! I NEED MORE CEREAL!

WANDA, DID YOU PICK UP MY JACKET FROM THE DRY CLEANER?

WHAT DO YOU MEAN WE DEPEND ON YOU TOO MUCH?

DADDY, TELL MOM I SPILLED MY MILK.

YOU REALLY THINK THAT WE DEPEND ON YOU TOO MUCH?

LOOK AROUND!

NOT ONLY DO I DO THE COOKING, CLEANING AND ORGANIZING AROUND HERE, I'M ALSO THE MAIN PROBLEM-SOLVER!

IF THERE'S A DISASTER, CALL **MOM**! IF THERE'S AN ERRAND TO BE RUN, CALL **MOM**! IF THERE'S A MESS TO BE CLEANED UP, AN APPOINTMENT TO KEEP, OR A DECISION TO BE MADE, CALL **MOM**!

WHAT DO YOU THINK WE SHOULD DO ABOUT THAT?

ALL I'M SAYING IS THAT I NEED A LITTLE RELIEF.

GOTCHA.

I'M TIRED OF BEING IN CHARGE OF EVERYTHING AROUND THE HOUSE, AND I NEED YOU AND ZOE TO PITCH IN AND TAKE A LITTLE MORE RESPONSIBILITY.

SAY NO MORE!

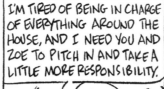

WE'LL START BY EMPTYING THE DISHWASHER FOR YOU!

THANKS, GUYS.... I REALLY APPRECIATE THE—

WHERE DO THESE BOWLS GO?

—EFFORT.

I CAN'T REACH THE COUNTER, SO I'LL JUST PUT THESE ON THE FLOOR, OKAY?

WHEW! THE KIDS ARE FINALLY IN BED!

YEAH.

CLICK!

THINGS ARE SO NOISY AND CHAOTIC WHEN I GET HOME FROM WORK THAT I REALLY LOOK FORWARD TO THE PART OF THE EVENING WHEN I CAN SIT AND TALK TO...

...MYSELF.

ZZZZZ

KIRKMAN & SCOTT

WATCH, DADDY! WATCH!

OKAY... I'M WATCHING!

WHUMP!

WOW! THAT WAS GREAT, ZOE! GOOD JOB! 'ATTA GIRL!

ACTUALLY, SHE JUST WANTED YOU TO SEE THE FIRST PART... THE FALLING WAS AN ACCIDENT.

OH...

THANKS A LOT, DAD.

KIRKMAN & SCOTT

BABY BLUES®
BY RICK KIRKMAN / JERRY SCOTT

THAT'S ENOUGH TV FOR TONIGHT, ZOE...YOU NEED TO DO SOMETHING ELSE FOR A WHILE.

BZZZT!

OKAY, LET'S PLAY CIRCUS!

YOU BE THE ELEPHANT, AND I'LL STAND ON YOUR BACK AND LOOK BEAUTIFUL.

GRUNT! WELL, OKAY...

NOW YOU WALK AROUND WHILE I DO TRICKS.

OW! OW! NO JUMPING!

TAG! YOU'RE IT!

BONK!

HEY!

YOU CAN'T CATCH MEEEE...

OH, YEAH? WE'LL SEE ABOUT TH—AAAAGH!

WHEEEEE!

NOOOOOO!

I THOUGHT DADDY DIDN'T WANT YOU TO WATCH ANY MORE TV TONIGHT.

HE CHANGED HIS MIND.

KIRKMAN & SCOTT

149

My daughter says "callipidder" instead of "caterpillar," and it's my fault. Unlike Darryl, I can't bring myself to correct her because it's just too darned cute. Sue me. —J.S.

Based on a trip to Disney World and Universal City in Florida one summer. 'Nuff said. —R.K.

Strip 1:

Panel 1: SEVEN HOURS OF DRIVING... SIX HOURS OF STANDING IN LINE... $79 WORTH OF SOUVENIRS... $16 FOR PARKING... AND FOR WHAT??

Panel 2: THANKS, DADDY. THAT WAS FUN. I LOVE YOU.

Panel 3: FOR THAT. / LET'S COME AGAIN TOMORROW.

KIRKMAN & SCOTT

Strip 2:

Panel 1: WAAAAAA!

Panel 5: YEAH, WELL, I CAN DO A SOMERSAULT, AND YOU CAN'T!

KIRKMAN & SCOTT

Strip 3:

Panel 1: WHEN I GROW UP I WANNA LIVE IN A BARBIE® HOUSE AN' HAVE A BARBIE® CAR AN' WEAR BARBIE® CLOTHES!

Panel 2: AN' I WANT A BARBIE® BEDROOM, AN' A BARBIE® KITCHEN, AN' A BARBIE® BATHROOM!

Panel 3: THAT'S ALL.?? DON'T YOU WANT MORE OUT OF LIFE, ZOE?

Panel 4: OH YEAH... AN' A BARBIE® BOAT! / ATTAGIRL... SHOOT FOR THE STARS!

KIRKMAN & SCOTT

LOOK! WE GOT ZOE'S PRESCHOOL CLASS PICTURES!

ISN'T THIS CUTE? THE KIDS TRADED PICTURES WITH EACH OTHER ALREADY!

WHY IS THAT KID CHEWING ON A SNEAKER?

THAT'S BRYAN THE DINOSAUR, AND HE'S ALWAYS HUNGRY.

AN' THAT'S KENNY THE PASTE-EATER...

"...GWEN THE SCREAMER, JAKE THE WHINER, JENNIFER THE GRABBER..."

DOES EVERY KID THERE HAVE A NICKNAME?

MEET ZOE THE FILM-WASTER.

WANT ONE?

Darryl and Wanda have always struggled to make ends meet. Just because they're cartoon characters doesn't mean they shouldn't have to live like the rest of us.

158

I like this strip a lot. For me it epitomizes the relationship my sisters and I had as kids. —J.S.

Around our house this was referred to as "going boneless." —R.K.

"Sun Scream" is another direct lift from my daughter's vocabulary. As a lifelong redhead, I think it's a far superior name for the stuff.
—J.S.

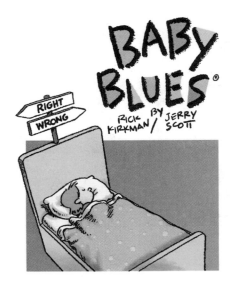

THE MORE BORED SHE GETS, THE MORE SHE RESEMBLES A THROW RUG.

I'D SAY OVERCOOKED SPAGHETTI.

MOM! MOM! MOM! MOM!

WHAT? WHAT IS IT, SWEETHEART?

DADDY AND I JUST SAW A GIANT YELLOW SNAKE **THIS** BIG!

WHAT? WHERE DID YOU SEE IT?

ON THE COUCH!

IS MOMMY GOING TO COME AND WATCH THE PYTHON SPECIAL WITH US?

SHE CAN'T. SHE'S ON THE ROOF WITH HAMMIE.

WHEN I GROW UP, I'M GOING TO RIDE MY BIKE ALL THE TIME!

WHEN I GROW UP, I'M GOING TO PLAY EVERY DAY!

WHEN I GROW UP, I'M GOING TO SING SONGS, EAT ICE CREAM AND DANCE WHENEVER I WANT TO!

ISN'T THAT INSPIRING?

I DON'T KNOW... WE'RE GROWN UP AND WE DON'T DO **ANY** OF THAT STUFF.

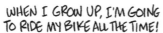

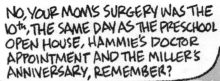

The "Golden-Haired Girl" is a real kid who terrorized and intimidated my daughter at preschool. I still don't know her real name. —J.S.

This part of the series is also a true story, although the names have been changed to protect the guilty. Our younger daughter informed us that she wanted to switch to her middle name after just such a situation on the first day of first grade. It had taken us the first four years of her life before we had stopped calling her by her older sister's name, and it was another couple of years before we finally could stop calling her by her first name.
—R.K.

171

BABY BLUES®

BY RICK KIRKMAN / JERRY SCOTT

OUR OWN BASKETBALL HOOP! THIS IS GOING TO BE **SO** COOL!

I CAN TEACH ZOE HOW TO DRIBBLE, HOW TO REBOUND... AND WHEN HAMMIE GETS BIG ENOUGH, WE CAN—

I THINK IT'S TOO HIGH.

BUT TEN FEET IS REGULATION.

HOW IS ZOE GOING TO BE ABLE TO GET THE BALL UP THERE?

OKAY, SO THE IDEA IS TO TOSS THE BALL THROUGH THE HOOP...

WAY UP **THERE??**

HMMM... OKAY... HOW'S THIS?

LOWER.

HERE?

MORE.

BUT...

MORE.

BUT...

RIGHT THERE! **PERFECT!** NOW IT'S FAIR!

SEE, ZOE? THESE ARE THE LETTERS OF THE ALPHABET!

YOU PUT THEM TOGETHER IN LITTLE GROUPS TO MAKE WORDS!

...BUT NOT **THAT** WORD...

WAS IT A GOOD ONE?

There was a period of time when the lower part of our refrigerator was covered with those little magnet letters that were constantly being rearranged by toddler hands. Occasionally some of those arrangements would spell real words, and sometimes those words weren't the kind you wanted to display to polite company. Proofreading the fridge became a necessary part of housekeeping. —J.S.

NOT AGAIN!

DOINK!

THAT'S OKAY. I WON'T FEEL BAD. I'LL DO BETTER NEXT TIME. EVERYBODY MAKES MISTAKES.

MAYBE WE'RE GOING A LITTLE HEAVY ON THE POSITIVE REINFORCEMENT.

I THINK AN EXTRA DESSERT WOULD HELP ME GET OVER THIS.

M-M-M-M-M-M-M-M-M...

MA-MA?

M-M-M-M-M-M-M-M-M-M-M...

ARE YOU TRYING TO SAY "MA-MA"? IT'S "MA-MA", ISN'T IT?

M-M-M-M-M-M-M-M-M...

IT'S "MA-MA"! IT'S "MA-MA"! IT'S "MA-MA"! IT'S "MA-MA"!

IT'S "MOTOR-CYCLE"!

⸚SIGH!⸚

M-M-M-M-M-M-M-M-M!

; SIGH! ; I CAN'T BELIEVE MY SON'S TRYING TO SAY "MOTORCYCLE" BEFORE HE SAYS "MA-MA."

I CARRIED HIM IN MY WOMB FOR NINE MONTHS... I GAVE **BIRTH** TO HIM... I FEED HIM FROM MY BREASTS, AND WHAT THANKS DO I GET??

I THINK HAMMIE JUST TRIED TO SAY "BAZOOKA"!

AAAAAAAGH!

I REALLY LOVE COMING HOME FROM WORK, WALKING THROUGH THE FRONT DOOR AND SEEING THE KIDS' FACES.

THERE'S NOTHING LIKE THOSE FOUR LITTLE WORDS EVERY FATHER YEARNS TO HEAR...

..."I LOVE YOU, DADDY!"

WHAT'D YOU BRING US?

OWWW! HE BIT ME!

CHOMP!

DON'T LET HIM GET AWAY WITH IT. YOU'RE SUPPOSED TO LOOK HIM STRAIGHT IN THE EYE AND GIVE HIM A FIRM "NO!"

NO!

DID IT WORK?

UH-UH.

BABY BLUES®

RICK BY JERRY
KIRKMAN / SCOTT

TWENTY-TWO...
TWENTY-THREE...
TWENTY-FOUR...

♪HA!HA!♪
TIME'S UP AND
♪YOU DIDN'T FIND
MEEEEEEE...EEEE!

OH, DARN!
YOU REALLY
FOOLED US
THAT TIME!

YEAH...
LET'S PLAY
AGAIN!

175

ZOE, I'M GOING TO THE HARDWARE STORE... WANT TO COME ALONG?

NO.

I'M ALSO GOING TO THE POST OFFICE, THE MARKET AND THE RECYCLING CENTER. ARE YOU SURE YOU DON'T WANT TO COME?

NO THANKS

OKAY, THEN... MAYBE I'LL JUST TAKE HAMMIE WITH ME.

DADDY'S PLAYING FAVORITES AGAIN!

KIRKMAN & SCOTT

LOOK, DADDY! I PAINTED YOU A PICTURE!

WOW!

SEE? THAT'S YOU AN' THAT'S ME, AN' THAT'S A RAINBOW!

THAT'S SO SWEET!

DON'T YOU JUST LOVE THIS? IT'S SO PURE... SO INNOCENT...

WHAT'S THAT LINE RIGHT THERE, ZOE?

MY COPYRIGHT.

KIRKMAN & SCOTT

ZOE! THE LEAVES ARE FALLING!

WHERE? I WANNA SEE!

WOW!

OOOH!

NEAT!

WASN'T THAT GREAT?

I THINK I LIKE TV BETTER.

KIRKMAN & SCOTT

BABY BLUES®
BY RICK KIRKMAN / JERRY SCOTT

GAAAAA! THESE STUPID PANTS ARE DRIVING ME **NUTS!**

WHAT'S WRONG WITH THEM?

ACTUALLY, NOTHING. IT'S ME. SOMEHOW I'VE GAINED FIVE POUNDS.

I CAN'T FIGURE IT OUT. NONE OF MY DIET OR EXERCISE HABITS HAVE CHANGED.

IN FACT, THE ONLY THING IN MY LIFE THAT'S DIFFERENT IS THAT ZOE IS GOING TO PRESCHOOL A COUPLE OF DAYS A WEEK!

I SEE...

SO ZOE'S BEEN GOING TO PRESCHOOL FOR ABOUT FIVE MONTHS, RIGHT?

YEAH. SO?

TWO DAYS A WEEK TIMES FOUR WEEKS IS EIGHT DAYS A MONTH, TIMES FIVE MONTHS IS 40 DAYS, RIGHT? SO IF ZOE TAKES ONE SANDWICH A DAY THAT AVERAGES FIVE OUNCES EACH, AND YOU...

WHAT? WHAT ARE YOU DOING?

KIRKMAN & SCOTT

ACCORDING TO MY FIGURES, YOU'RE WEARING FIVE POUNDS OF PEANUT BUTTER AND JELLY SANDWICH CRUSTS ON YOUR HIPS.

ET TU, SKIPPY?

OKAY, ZOE... GO!

OW!

WHY'D YOU KICK ME??

THAT'S MY FAVORITE BALL.

KIRKMAN & SCOTT

WHAT DO YOU WANT TO BE FOR HALLOWEEN, ZOE?

A SLUG.

A SLUG?? YOU MEAN A SNAIL?

NOT A SNAIL, A SLUG.

BUT SLUGS CRAWL ALONG THE GROUND LEAVING A TRAIL OF YUCKY SLIME....

HOW ARE YOU GOING TO LEAVE A TRAIL OF SLIME?

I'LL BRING HAMMIE.

KIRKMAN & SCOTT

GUESS WHAT YOUR DAUGHTER WANTS TO BE FOR HALLOWEEN.

A WITCH?   No

A CLOWN?   NO,

A PUPPY DOG?   NO,

A KITTY CAT?   NO,

A GHOST,   NO,

A GOBLIN,   NO,

A VAMPIRE?   NO,

KIRKMAN & SCOTT

A SLUG.

NO!

Once, as we were signing our daughter in to a kids play area at a mall, I had this great idea for a similar place where shopping-impaired dads could relax in recliners and watch big-screen TVs while their spouses shopped. If I had followed through on it, I'd probably be rich by now. —J.S.

This is a really effective strip. By leaving the border off, the stacks of clean laundry are emphasized and give the impression of disarray.

185

This comes from a couple of chronic nondancers.

187

ZOE! WHAT ARE YOU DOING IN HAMMIE'S CRIB?

PROTECTING HIM.

HE GOT AFRAID LAST NIGHT AND WANTED ME TO COME SLEEP IN HERE, SO I DID.

THAT WAS VERY BRAVE OF YOU.

WHAT WAS HE AFRAID OF?

THE MONSTERS UNDER MY BED.

READ ME A STORY, DADDY.

SURE, SWEETIE... WHICH ONE?

READ ME THE ONE ABOUT THE LITTLE GIRL WHO GOES TO THE BEACH AND FINDS THE MAGIC SHELL AND THE SEA FAIRY HELPS HER FIND HER LOST PUPPY AND THEY LIVE HAPPILY EVER AFTER.

IF YOU ALREADY KNOW THE STORY, WHY DO YOU WANT ME TO READ IT AGAIN?

SO I CAN LET YOU KNOW WHEN YOU MAKE MISTAKES.

HERE, DAD, I DREW ANOTHER PICTURE FOR YOU.

WOW.

GOSH, ZOE, YOU'VE DRAWN A LOT OF PICTURES FOR ME SINCE I GOT HOME FROM WORK TODAY! I'M REALLY LUCKY!

BUT MAYBE IT SHOULD BE MOMMY'S TURN FOR A WHILE.

THAT'S OKAY... I'VE BEEN THIS LUCKY ALREADY TODAY.

And all these little green hearts I'm giving you mean I love you very much!

Those aren't hearts... they're dollars.

Interpreting kids' drawings can be an eye-opening experience.

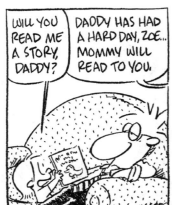

195

The Twelve Days of *Christmas*

On the first day of
Christmas my children
gave to me

A cartridge in a
fir tree.

The Twelve Days of *Christmas*

On the second day of
Christmas my children
gave to me
Two snotty gloves,
And a cartridge in a
fir tree.

The Twelve Days of *Christmas*

On the third day of
Christmas my children
gave to me
Three drenched friends,
Two snotty gloves,
And a cartridge in a
fir tree.

The Twelve Days of *Christmas*

On the fourth day of
Christmas my children
gave to me
Four appalling words,
Three drenched friends,
Two snotty gloves,
And a cartridge in a fir tree.

The Twelve Days of *Christmas*

On the fifth day of Christmas my children
gave to me
Five dozen **SCREAMS!**
Four appalling words,
Three drenched friends,
Two snotty gloves,
And a cartridge in a fir tree.

This parody of "The Twelve Days of Christmas" drew all sorts of responses.

Dear Baby Blues Cartoonists,

My husband went to three different stores and for some reason either they sold out of the paper or it had not been delivered yet. I wondered if you could possibly send a copy of the third and fourth days of Christmas.

Dear Writer of Baby Blues Comic Strip,

I am writing to voice my opinion on your 12 Days of Christmas comic strip. I find this comic to be repulsive and shows a considerable amount of disrespect to your readers.

197

The Twelve Days of *Christmas*

On *the sixth day of Christmas my children gave to me*

Six teeth decaying,
Five dozen **SCREAMS!**
Four appalling words,
Three drenched friends,
Two snotty gloves,
And a cartridge in a fir tree.

The Twelve Days of *Christmas*

On *the seventh day of Christmas my children gave to me*

Seven tons of washing,
Six teeth decaying,
Five dozen **SCREAMS!**
Four appalling words,

Three drenched friends,
Two snotty gloves,
And a cartridge in a fir tree.

The Twelve Days of *Christmas*

On *the eighth day of Christmas my children gave to me*

Eight ways of belching,
Seven tons of washing,
Six teeth decaying,
Five dozen **SCREAMS!**

Four appalling words,
Three drenched friends,
Two snotty gloves,
And a cartridge in a fir tree.

The Twelve Days of *Christmas*

On the ninth day of Christmas my children gave to me

Nine songs they can't sing,
Eight ways of belching,
Seven tons of washing,
Six teeth decaying,
Five dozen **SCREAMS!**

Four appalling words,
Three drenched friends,
Two snotty gloves,
And a cartridge in a fir tree.

The Twelve Days of *Christmas*

On the tenth day of Christmas my children gave to me

Ten Fords a-beeping,
Nine songs they can't sing,
Eight ways of belching,
Seven tons of washing,
Six teeth decaying,

Five dozen **SCREAMS!**
Four appalling words,
Three drenched friends,
Two snotty gloves,
And a cartridge in a fir tree.

The Twelve Days of *Christmas*

On the eleventh day of Christmas my children gave to me

Eleven diaper wipings,
Ten Fords a-beeping,
Nine songs they can't sing,
Eight ways of belching,
Seven tons of washing,
Six teeth decaying,

Five dozen **SCREAMS!**
Four appalling words,
Three drenched friends,
Two snotty gloves,
And a cartridge in a fir tree.

The Twelve Days of Christmas

On the twelfth day of Christmas my children gave to me

Twelve plumbers plumbing,
Eleven diaper wipings,
Ten Fords a-beeping,
Nine songs they can't sing,
Eight ways of belching,
Seven tons of washing,

Six teeth decaying,
Five dozen **SCREAMS!**
Four appalling words,
Three drenched friends,
Two snotty gloves,
And a cartridge in a fir tree.

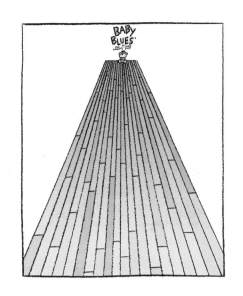

READY, HAMMIE?

ON YOUR MARK... GET SET...

GO!

THE KIDS SEEM TO BE PLAYING TOGETHER NICELY FOR A CHANGE.

YEAH. IT'S NICE TO SEE ZOE TAKE AN INTEREST IN HER LITTLE BROTHER...

FASTER! FASTER! GO! GO!

...EVEN IF IT IS ONLY AS A PIECE OF SPORTING EQUIPMENT.

STRIKE!!

KIRKMAN & SCOTT

205

BABY BLUES®

Rick by Jerry
Kirkman / Scott

FOUR GREAT MYTHS OF PARENTING

MYTH 1

THE MOST IMPORTANT THING FOR A PARENT TO POSSESS IS PATIENCE.

REALITY

THE MOST IMPORTANT THING FOR A PARENT TO POSSESS IS AN EXTRA SET OF CAR KEYS!

JUST TRY TO REMEMBER WHERE YOU PUT THEM, OKAY? **PLEEEEEASE?**

MYTH 2

TAKING LOTS OF PICTURES OF YOUR BABY WILL FILL YOUR LIVES WITH MEMORIES.

REALITY

TAKING LOTS OF PICTURES OF YOUR BABY WILL FILL YOUR **CLOSETS** WITH MEMORIES!

JUST A LITTLE HARDER... WE ALMOST HAD IT!

MAYBE WE SHOULD GET SOME PHOTO ALBUMS.

MYTH 3

A GOOD BABY SITTER IS WORTH HER WEIGHT IN GOLD.

REALITY

A GOOD BABY SITTER **CHARGES** HER WEIGHT IN GOLD!

THAT'S OKAY... I TAKE MASTERCARD, VISA AND AMERICAN EXPRESS...

KIRKMAN & SCOTT

MYTH 4

TWO CHILDREN AREN'T REALLY MUCH MORE WORK THAN ONE.

REALITY

YEAH. RIGHT.

HA! HA! HAAAAAA! SNORT! **WA**-HAA-HAAA! HAHAHAHA!

Tip for new dads: This actually works pretty well.

213

HERE, DADDY. THIS IS FOR YOU. IT'S A SIGN.

OH. THANKS. VERY NICE.

I'LL TELL YOU WHAT... WHY DON'T YOU KEEP IT FOR ME SO I DON'T LOSE IT?

IT SAYS, "I LOVE DADDY BECAUSE HE'S THE BEST DADDY IN THE WORLD AND I MEAN IT, SO **THERE**! LOVE, ZOE."

KIRKMAN & SCOTT

Toddlers are born lawyers.

NO DESSERT UNLESS YOU FINISH YOUR VEGETABLES.

I'M DONE.

I'LL EAT **ONE** BITE.

FIVE BITES.

THREE BITES, AN' I'LL DRINK ALL OF MY MILK, TOO.

FOUR BITES, THE MILK, **AND** YOU TAKE YOUR PLATE TO THE SINK WHEN YOU'RE FINISHED.

DEAL!

ARE WE SENDING HER TO PRESCHOOL OR **LAW** SCHOOL?

AN' THIS COUNTS AS A BITE.

KIRKMAN & SCOTT

HARRUMPH! GOTTA GO TO WORK! GOTTA PAY BILLS! BYE-BYE, KIDS!

HA! HA! HA! HA! THAT'S A GREAT IMPRESSION OF DADDY!

I DON'T SOUND LIKE THAT!

SURE YOU DO! DON'T BE SO SENSITIVE!

OKAY, **NOW** GUESS WHO I AM!

YOU KIDS ARE DRIVING ME NUTS! I ONLY HAVE TWO HANDS! GET IN HERE AN' PICK THAT UP!

OOH! I HAVE A GUESS!

THIS HAD BETTER BE GRANDMA...

KIRKMAN & SCOTT

215

I'LL BE RIGHT BACK...I'M JUST GOING TO PUT THE TRASH CAN OUT.

OKAY.

I WANNA GO!

MY TURN! MY TURN!

ZOE, LET DADDY DO THE PUSHING! IT'S TOO BIG FOR YOU!

WHEEEEEE!

BE CAREFUL! SLOW DOWN! DON'T TIP TH—

ALL FINISHED?

OH YES.

AN' I HELPED!

HI, SIS... COME ON IN.

WHERE'S THE CHEESECAKE?

SO, HOW ARE YOU DOING?

HE IS AN INSECT! AN EMOTIONAL AMOEBA!

MEN ARE NOTHING BUT A BUNCH OF BRAINLESS, TESTOSTERONE-SOAKED CRETINS!

THAT WOULD BE YOUR CUE TO LEAVE.

OKAY... I'LL TRY NOT TO SCRAPE MY KNUCKLES ON THE FLOOR ON MY WAY OUT.

BYE, SIS... I'LL CALL YOU TOMORROW.

SO, IS RHONDA ALL RIGHT?

SHE'S FINE. IT'S ALWAYS A CRISIS WHEN SHE BREAKS UP WITH A BOYFRIEND.

I'M SO GLAD WE'RE MARRIED AND PAST ALL THAT DATING NONSENSE.

YEAH. IT'S NICE TO KNOW THAT NO MATTER WHAT I SAY OR DO, WE'LL END UP IN BED TOGETHER AT THE END OF THE EVENING.

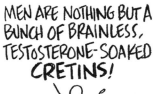

219

COME ON, HAMMIE...
SAY "MA-MA."

I'LL SAY IT FOR HIM.
"MA-MA."

NO, ZOE... I WANT HIM
TO SAY IT HIMSELF.

WHY?

BECAUSE HE HAS TO LEARN TO
TALK SO HE CAN TELL US
THINGS LIKE WHAT HE'S
THINKING, WHAT HE NEEDS
AND WHAT HE WANTS...

KIRKMAN & SCOTT

NOW, SAY
"MA-MA"...

I THOUGHT
THAT'S WHAT
I WAS HERE
FOR!

Parenting
lesson
No. 112
"When to worry"

EVERYTHING
IS FINE!
DON'T WORRY!

THIS IS MY
FAVORITE PICTURE
OF US.

YOU'VE GOT
TO BE
KIDDING!

LOOK... BOTH KIDS ARE CRYING,
THE WIND IS BLOWING OUR HAIR ALL
OVER THE PLACE, MY TONGUE IS
STICKING OUT AND WE'RE BOTH
SQUINTING FROM THE SUN!

HOW CAN THIS
BE YOUR
FAVORITE PICTURE?

I
LOOK
SKINNY.

KIRKMAN & SCOTT

222

WATCH OUT!

WHA—?

YOU ALMOST SAT ON **NADINE!**

WHO??

NADINE, ZOE'S NEW INVISIBLE FRIEND. SHE LIVES UNDER THE PATIO, WEARS POLKA DOTS AND PIGTAILS AND ONLY EATS CHEESE.

CAN YOU RUN THAT BY ME AGAIN?

AAAGH! HER HEAD!

It was years before my wife and I knew that our younger daughter had imaginary friends. Her sister had known about them all along. One such friend was from Neptune. I'd better not say any more. . . . —R.K.

ZOE HAS AN INVISIBLE FRIEND? SINCE WHEN?

I DON'T KNOW... ABOUT A WEEK.

IT'S OKAY, NADINE... MY DADDY DIDN'T MEAN TO SIT ON YOUR HEAD.

WHY DIDN'T YOU TELL ME ABOUT THIS?

I GUESS I JUST FORGOT TO MENTION IT.

HE'S USUALLY A LOT MORE CAREFUL.

I'M **ALWAYS** THE LAST TO KNOW ANYTHING AROUND HERE.

AIEEEEEE! HE DID IT AGAIN!

MOM, NADINE WANTS SOME CHOCOLATE MILK.

TELL YOUR INVISIBLE FRIEND THAT IT'S ALMOST DINNERTIME.

SO?

SO CHOCOLATE MILK WILL SPOIL NADINE'S APPETITE AND SHE WON'T WANT TO EAT HER DINNER.

NADINE SAYS THAT SHE DOESN'T CARE BECAUSE SHE DOESN'T LIKE THE WAY YOU COOK ANYWAY.

ME AND YOUR BIG MOUTH!

223

ZOE, WHAT DID YOU GUYS DO TODAY?

LOTS OF STUFF!

I MADE MACARONI NECKLACES, I GLUED MACARONI ON PAPER TO MAKE PICTURES, WE PLAYED MACARONI BINGO...

WOW! NEAT! YOU'RE REALLY LUCKY!

IF YOU THINK **THAT** SOUNDED LIKE FUN, WAIT UNTIL YOU HEAR WHAT WE'RE HAVING FOR DINNER.

WAIT! MAKE HIM GUESS!

KIRKMAN & SCOTT

KNOCK! KNOCK!

WHO'S THERE?

NOBODY!

SHRIEK! HA! HA! HA! HA! HA! HA!

KIRKMAN & SCOTT

MULTIPLY THAT BY A THOUSAND, AND YOU HAVE A PRETTY GOOD IDEA OF WHAT **MY** DAY WAS LIKE.

KNOCK! KNOCK!

HI, HONEY. WOW! YOU LOOK **GREAT**!

MMMMMM... YOU **SMELL** GREAT, TOO!

I THINK IT'S REALLY SEXY THAT YOU SHOWERED AND CHANGED CLOTHES JUST BEFORE I GOT HOME FROM WORK.

KIRKMAN & SCOTT

SEXY-SCHMEXY... IT WAS THE FIRST CHANCE I HAD TO GET INTO THE BATHROOM TODAY!

This strip wasn't
by any one even
actually represer
honest look at ho
handle gooey em
around the house. —J.S.

227

ZOE, I MADE YOU A PEANUT BUTTER AND JELLY SANDWICH, APPLE SLICES, CARROT STICKS AND MILK FOR YOUR LUNCH, OKAY?

OKAY.

EXCEPT INSTEAD OF PEANUT BUTTER AN' JELLY, I WANT TURKEY... AN' CELERY INSTEAD OF CARROTS... AN' PEACHES, NOT APPLES.

GOOD GUESS ON THE MILK, THOUGH.

OKAY...HERE'S THE NUCLEAR SUBMARINE PR—

A **BARBIE®** SUBMARINE.

RIGHT, HERE'S THE **BARBIE®** NUCLEAR SUBMARINE PROWLING OFF THE ALASKAN COAST WHEN A GIANT SQUID SUD—

A **PINK BARBIE®** SUBMARINE, WITH FLOWERS.

AN' THE SQUID'S NAME IS BRENDA.

FINE! THE PINK BARBIE® SUBMARINE WITH FLOWERS IS PROWLING OFF THE ALASKAN COAST WHEN A GIANT SQUID NAMED BRENDA SHOWS UP. **THEN** WHAT?

I DON'T KNOW... IT'S **YOUR** STORY.

AWWWW...

DARRYL! YOU HAVE TO COME AND SEE THIS!

ISN'T THAT SOMETHING?

YEAH...

...ARE THEY SLEEPING, OR DID THEY FINALLY KNOCK EACH OTHER COLD?

I'M BACK!

DID YOU GET THE PICTURES?

YOU BET.

OOOH! I LOVE PORTRAITS! DID THEY COME OUT GOOD?

WELL, THAT DEPENDS ON YOUR POINT OF VIEW...

...IT LOOKS JUST LIKE THEM, IF THAT'S WHAT YOU MEAN.

HAMMIE IS GOING TO BE A **YEAR** OLD NEXT MONTH!

REALLY?

CAN WE HAVE A PARTY? AN' WEAR FUNNY HATS? AN' EAT CAKE? AN' OPEN PRESENTS?

SURE!

ABSOLUTELY...

...BUT REMEMBER THAT IT'S HAMMIE'S BIRTHDAY, SO ALL OF THE PRESENTS WILL BE FOR HIM.

ALL OF THEM?

WHAT KIND OF PARTY IS **THAT**?

MOM, WHAT TIME IS IT?

IT'S TIME FOR THE WHISTLING MONKEY COWBOY BAND TV SHOW.

MOM, WHAT TIME IS IT NOW?

IT'S TIME FOR SESAME STREET.

WHAT TIME IS IT, MOM?

IT'S FIFTEEN MINUTES UNTIL THE STORYBOOK SHOW.

WHY DO WE EVEN HAVE A CLOCK ANYMORE?

231

I have an E-mail pal who is a pediatrician in Pennsylvania. She has a great sense of humor and she sends me funny stories about her daughter or patients that occasionally turn into *Baby Blues* strips. I think this came from an incident with her daughter. —J.S.

WOW! HIS WALKING ISN'T SO GOOD, BUT HIS **WRECKS** ARE SPECTACULAR!

REAL SENSITIVE, DARRYL.

KIRKMAN & SCOTT

After our kids got past the preschool years, our sick days dropped about tenfold. Our pediatrician writes occasionally to say he misses us (either that, or he has a boat payment due). —R.K.

BABY BLUES®

BY RICK KIRKMAN / JERRY SCOTT

YOU LOOK TIRED, SWEETIE.

DO I?

HMMM...THAT'S FUNNY. ALL I DID WAS BREAST-FEED AND CARE FOR A BABY, AND PICK UP AFTER A FOUR YEAR-OLD ALL DAY.

AND I ONLY WASHED SIX LOADS OF LAUNDRY, PREPARED BREAKFAST, LUNCH AND DINNER, MADE 25 FUND-RAISING CALLS FOR THE PRE-SCHOOL AND WENT GROCERY SHOPPING WITH TWO SCREAMING KIDS.

SILLY ME! I'LL TRY TO LOOK **PERKIER** FOR YOU AT THE END OF THE DAY **TOMORROW**!

TIRED? DID I SAY "TIRED"?

I MEANT **CONTENT**! AND **ACCOMPLISHED**! YES SIR! CONTENT, ACCOMPLISHED AND TOTALLY TOGETHER. THAT'S YOU!

REALLY?

ABSOLUTELY! YOU BET!

THAT'S BETTER.

PLUS, YOUR VARICOSE VEINS AREN'T LOOKING TOO BAD TODAY, EITHER!

235

236

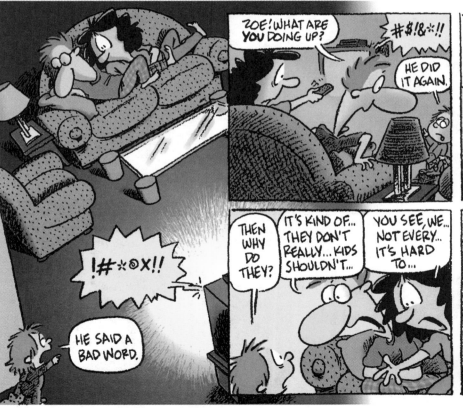

Our nephews: heavy equipment fanatics from day one.
—R.K.

WHAT'S THAT?

IT'S A BIRTHDAY PRESENT FOR HAMMIE.

I BROUGHT HIM SOME BULLDOZER PAJAMAS... AREN'T THEY CUTE?

EWWWWWW! YUK! BULLDOZERS!

BULLDOZERS ARE FOR BOYS! BULLDOZERS ARE BORING! ICK! BLEAH! EWWWW!

DID YOU GET ME SOME, TOO?

IS HAMMIE GONNA HAVE A BIRTHDAY PARTY LIKE ME?

YES...ON APRIL TWENTY-NINTH, REMEMBER?

WITH CAKE AND ICE CREAM, TOO?

THAT'S RIGHT.

DON'T WORRY...FROM NOW ON, YOU AND HAMMIE WILL EACH HAVE ONE BIRTHDAY EVERY YEAR WITH EQUAL-SIZED CAKES, AN EQUAL AMOUNT OF ICE CREAM, AND AN EQUAL NUMBER OF PRESENTS.

YES.

REALLY?

NO FAIR!!

I THINK THERE ARE GOING TO BE LOTS OF BALLOONS AT YOUR BIRTHDAY PARTY, HAMMIE!

BNNZ!

AN' CAKE.., AN' ICE CREAM... AN' KIDS... AN' PRESENTS...

UNH! UNH! UNH!

TOO BAD YOU CAN'T COME...

WAAAAAAAAAAA

WHAT HAPPENED?

AAAAAAAAAAA!

HE'S PROBABLY JUST TIRED.

KIRKMAN & SCOTT

239

Although Wanda is admirably breast-feeding longer than most women do in this country, we still show that there's some part of her that tires of it. Breast-feeding advocates alternate between loving us and hating us for our depiction of nursing mothers. They did both over this one.

This came from a question from our teenage daughter, curious about the effects of hole punchers on hair. Sometimes you just have to wonder about how their brains are wired. . . .
—R.K.

Panel 1: DARRYL, WHAT DO YOU THINK ABOUT JUST KEEPING HAMMIE'S FIRST BIRTHDAY PARTY SMALL?
FINE WITH ME.

Panel 2: YOU KNOW... MAYBE JUST THE THREE OF US AND MY SISTER.
SOUNDS GOOD.

Panel 3: I MEAN, WHAT'S THE POINT OF MAKING A BIG DEAL OUT OF IT? HE'S STILL A BABY, AND WE DON'T WANT TO OVERSTIMULATE HIM, AND BESIDES...
WHOA! HEY! TIME OUT! I **SAID** I **AGREED** WITH YOU!

Panel 4: YOU DON'T HAVE TO SELL **ME** ON THE IDEA.
I KNOW... I WAS JUST TRYING TO CONVINCE MY CONSCIENCE.

Panel 5: WHAT KIND OF CAKE DO YOU THINK HAMMIE WOULD LIKE FOR HIS BIRTHDAY?

Panel 6: I KNOW! IT SHOULD BE HIS FAVORITE FLAVOR!
THAT'S A GOOD IDEA.

Panel 7: (wordless)

Panel 8: WAIT... I DON'T THINK THEY MAKE BREAST-MILK-FLAVORED CAKE MIX.
TOO BAD.

Panel 9: HAPPY BIRTHDAY TO YOU! HAPPY BIRTHDAY TO YOU! HAPPY BIRTHDAY, DEAR HAMMIE! HAPPY BIRTHDAY TO YOOOOU!
THIP THIP THIP THIP

Panel 10: OKAY, HAMMIE... BLOW OUT THE CANDLE! COME ON... BLOW!
BLOW!
THIP THIP THIP

Panel 11: BURRRP!

Panel 12: DOES HE STILL GET HIS WISH?
I THINK HE JUST DID.

KIRKMAN & SCOTT

NEVER HAVE SO MANY WORKED SO HARD FOR SO LITTLE.

AT LEAST, NOT SINCE THE **LAST** BIRTHDAY PARTY.

REALLY.

YOU MEAN IT'S OVER ALREADY??

Z

KIRKMAN & SCOTT

SO WE'RE OFFICIALLY THE PARENTS OF A ONE-YEAR-OLD AND AN ALMOST FOUR-YEAR-OLD.

I CAN'T BELIEVE IT.

IT'S MINE! GIVE IT TO ME! GIVE IT! GIVE IT! NAH! NAH! BWAAAAAA!

OKAY... **NOW I CAN.**

KIRKMAN & SCOTT

GIRLS ARE **BETTER** THAN BOYS! NEYAAH!

HEE! HEE!

I CAN'T BELIEVE YOU'RE LAUGHING AT THIS.

OH, COME ON...

GIRLS ARE **PRETTIER** THAN BOYS!

...THEY'RE JUST PLAYING. DON'T TAKE IT SO SERIOUSLY!

MOMMIES ARE **SMARTER** THAN DADDIES!

MAYBE YOU'RE RIGHT.

HEY!

KIRKMAN & SCOTT

My daughter cherishes *every* piece of artwork that she creates, so we have to clean out closets and drawers under the cover of darkness. —J.S.

LOOK! HAMMIE IS WALKING ALL BY HIMSELF AGAIN!

WOW!

YAY! HE'S WALKING! YIPPEE! YIPPEE! **YIPPEE!**

I THINK ZOE IS MORE EXCITED ABOUT HAMMIE WALKING THAN EITHER OF US.

I KNOW, KIND OF SWEET, ISN'T IT?

HAMMIE, GO GET ME MY DOLL.

KIRKMAN & SCOTT

WHAT ARE YOU COOKING?

CHICKEN AND RICE.

CHICKEN AND RICE?? EWWWWWW!

BLEAH! **YUK!** GAAAAAK!

KIRKMAN & SCOTT

WHAT'S THAT TASTE LIKE?

DIAPER CHANGING, BREAST-FEEDING, POTTY TRAINING, RUNNY NOSES—

THEY ALL ADD UP TO ONE BIG QUESTION...

KIRKMAN & SCOTT

...IS THERE LIFE AFTER BIRTH?

247

A very faithful reproduction of one of our kids' drawings. —R.K.

 MOM! DAD! COME QUICK!

 HURRY! HURRY! SEE! SEE!

 FOR HEAVEN'S SAKE, ZOE! HAMMIE ISN'T "FREAKING OUT!"... HE HAS THE HICCUPS!

WHERE DID YOU HEAR THE TERM, "FREAKING OUT," ANYWAY?

HIC! HIC! HIC! HIC!

OH, TOO BAD.

 LOOK, DADDY! I'M WALKING HAMMIE!

THAT'S GREAT, ZOE!

 SEE? HE GOES WHEREVER I WANT HIM TO GO... AROUND THE CHAIR... PAST THE COUCH... BY THE TABLE—

 BONK!

 INTO THE WALL...

THAT ONE WAS HIS IDEA.

 WE NEED A BIGGER HOUSE.

YEAH...

 ...OR, WE COULD JUST WORK REALLY HARD AT KEEPING THINGS ORGANIZED AND CLEAN SO THIS PLACE WOULD SEEM A WHOLE LOT BIGGER.

YEAH...

 EEEEEEEEEEEEE!

 IT WOULD BE EASIER TO GET A NEW HOUSE, THOUGH.

YEAH.

NOW, YOU AND HAMMIE BE GOOD FOR KIKI.

WE WILL.

LISTEN TO WHAT SHE SAYS... PICK UP YOUR TOYS WHEN YOU'RE FINISHED PLAYING WITH THEM... DON'T MAKE A MESS... USE YOUR INSIDE VOICES...

IN OTHER WORDS, JUST ACT THE OPPOSITE OF THE WAY YOU ACT FOR ME.

WE ALWAYS DO!

KIRKMAN & SCOTT

I'M GLAD YOU'RE BABY-SITTING US, KIKI.

THANKS, ZOE!

BYE, GUYS!

KIKI IS A REALLY GOOD BABYSITTER, HAMMIE, YOU'LL LIKE HER, IT'S JUST LIKE HAVING MOMMY WITH US...

...EXCEPT LESS CRABBY.

I HEARD THAT!

KIRKMAN & SCOTT

HEY, ZOE! LET'S SEE HOW MUCH YOU WEIGH.

I CAN DO IT MYSELF... MOMMY SHOWED ME HOW.

AAAAAUGH!

KIRKMAN & SCOTT

DID I DO IT RIGHT, MOMMY?

I THINK IT'S TIME FOR ONE OF OUR "DO AS I SAY, NOT AS I DO" LESSONS,

BABY BLUES®
BY RICK KIRKMAN / JERRY SCOTT

♪

HEY-Y-Y-Y! WOW! HAVE YOU BEEN SHOPPING TODAY?

THOSE COLORS LOOK **GOOD** ON YOU! NICE! TRÉS CHIC. VER·R·Y HIP.

I DIDN'T EVEN KNOW THEY **MADE** MOTHER-DAUGHTER CAMOUFLAGE SUN DRESSES.

VERY FUNNY. NEXT TIME, **YOU'RE** FEEDING HIM THE STRAINED BEEF AND VEGETABLES.

INCOMING!

KIRKMAN & SCOTT

Rick and Jerry!

I can't wait till they (Darryl and Wanda) have another baby cause you drew the baby so tiny but so correct and I felt it was my own child.

My children, when young, pulled the same things as your children in the strip do and I find myself nodding my head and saying, "Yes, I remember."

Congrats to two wonderful artists.

A.M.V.

Dear Baby Blues cartoonists,

It may be that your comic strip is the reason I am single, have no plans for marriage, and may be getting a vasectomy in the near future.

Thank you.

Via Internet